W9-DJL-031

1001 little ways
to save the planet

1001 little ways to save the planet

Esme Floyd

METRO BOOKS
NEW YORK

Text and design copyright © 2007
Carlton Books Limited
Illustrations copyright © 2007 Carol Morley

This 2008 edition published by Metro Books
by arrangement with Carlton Books Limited

All rights reserved. No part of this book may be reproduced,
stored in a retrieval system, or transmitted, in any form or
by any means, electronic, mechanical, photocopying,
recording, or otherwise, without prior written permission
from the publisher.

Executive Editor: Lisa Dyer
Senior Art Editor: Zoë Dissell
Design: Liz Wiffen
Copy Editor: Carla Masson
Illustrator: Carol Morley
Production: Caroline Alberti

Metro Books
122 Fifth Avenue
New York, NY 10011

ISBN 13: 978-1-4351-0198-2
ISBN 10: 1-4351-0198-7

Printed and bound in Dubai

10 9 8 7 6 5 4 3 2 1

This book reports information and opinions which may be
of general interest to the reader. Neither the author nor the
publisher can accept responsibility for any accident, injury,
or damage that results from using the ideas, information, or
advice offered in this book.

CONTENTS

introduction   **6**

home help   **8**

interiors   **60**

gardening   **94**

at work   **122**

lifestyle   **140**

family life   **196**

the environment   **208**

index   **222**

INTRODUCTION

We all know how important it is to think about the effect our everyday lives have on the environment, but often we feel we just don't have time to make those all-important changes. Not any more—this book has done all the hard work for you, giving you simple tips to help reduce the damage you're doing to the planet.

For example, did you know that simply replacing a plastic lunchbox with a metal one will help reduce greenhouse gas emissions, or that recycling garbage bags could reduce your volume of waste by 20%? This book is packed with simple, easy-to-follow hints and helpers that will set you on the way to becoming a greener citizen. Not only are the tips good for the environment, they're easy on your pocket, too. So get reading now, and start making those little changes sooner rather than later.

Top ten little ways to save the planet

190
STOP THE DRIP
(see Utilities, page 48)

194
CHANGE YOUR BULBS
(see Utilities, page 49)

380
CATCH THE WAVE
(see Kitchens, page 88)

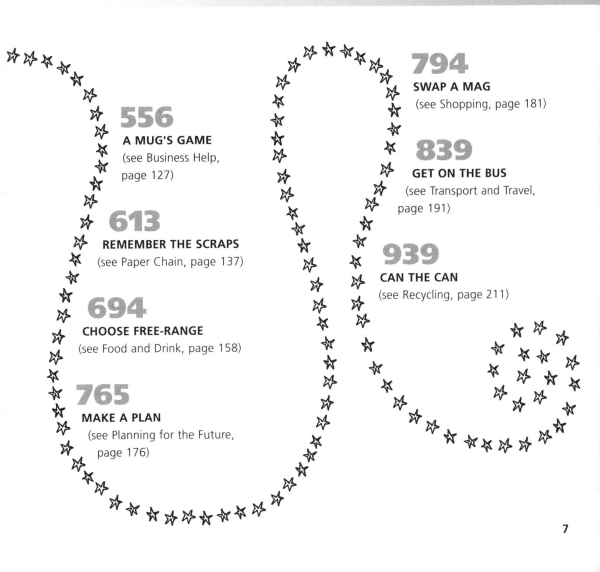

556
A MUG'S GAME
(see Business Help,
page 127)

613
REMEMBER THE SCRAPS
(see Paper Chain, page 137)

694
CHOOSE FREE-RANGE
(see Food and Drink, page 158)

765
MAKE A PLAN
(see Planning for the Future,
page 176)

794
SWAP A MAG
(see Shopping, page 181)

839
GET ON THE BUS
(see Transport and Travel,
page 191)

939
CAN THE CAN
(see Recycling, page 211)

cleaning

1 POLISH YOUR OWN

Instead of using furniture polish in an aerosol can, make your own totally natural polish using beeswax, turpentine, and your favorite essential oil to make your house smell as well as look good.

2 SALT YOUR SILVER

Silver cleaners can be abrasive and harsh. Make your own cleaner for sterling (not plate) silver by mixing 1 pint of water with a teaspoon each of salt and baking powder and adding a strip of aluminum foil. Drop the silver into this mixture, boil for a few minutes, remove with tongs and polish with a soft cloth. Add lemon juice for really grimy silver.

3 DON'T DISPOSE

Instead of disposable dishcloths that have to be thrown away and replaced every few weeks, choose cotton cloths. They'll stand the test of time and can be washed and reused for many months.

4 SAY RHUBARB TO DIRTY PANS

Degreasers designed to clean your kitchen pans are often full of harsh and toxic ingredients. You can clean the bottom of your pan without resorting to chemicals by boiling some rhubarb in the pan, which will pull the dirt off the sides (except on aluminum, where you should use vinegar).

5 DUST YOUR BULBS

Don't stop at dusting your mantelpieces and shelves—keeping your light bulbs dust free could help save energy as it will increase output, making them more efficient.

6 DISINFECT NATURALLY

Not only do disinfectants contain harsh chemicals that are damaging to the environment, they smell strong, too. Make your own natural disinfectant by infusing leaves of rosemary, eucalyptus, lavender, sage, and thyme in water.

7 CUT DOWN YOUR PRODUCTS

Did you know that more bleach and detergent are released into the environment from household waste than during their manufacturing process? Cut down on the use of bleach and detergent whenever you can. For example, a scrub of cold water and table salt, applied with a cloth or scourer, works as well as bleach on cutlery and cutting boards.

8 GO LARGE

Don't buy a new plastic spray pump every time you need a refill. Instead, buy cleaning products in the largest possible containers and refill your plastic containers as you need to. There are other products you can get in bulk and decant so you won't be buying unnecessary packaging, such as food items like spices or rice or health-and-beauty products like shampoo or body wash.

9 GREASE IT OUT

Don't smother kitchen grease in increasingly powerful detergents, which are toxic to the environment. First, try a simple mixture of salt and baking soda. When mixed together, these two have powerful degreasing properties, without causing any harm to the environment.

10 SPRINKLE AWAY SMELLS

Instead of using room fresheners or anti-smell powders and sprays in your garbage can to cut down on nasty odors, simply sprinkle a handful of salt inside. The salt acts by neutralizing unwanted smells.

11 HANDS OFF SMELLS

If your hands smell of fish or onions after preparing a meal, don't immediately reach for the hand-washing liquid. Salt dissolved in warm water will do just as well as a handwash and will keep your run-off water detergent-free.

12 BREW UP A CLEAN FLOOR

Tea is all you need to clean wooden floors and bring up the shine, particularly on older wooden flooring. Brew two teabags in hot water and cool to room temperature, then apply with a mop or a cloth. The added bonus is that there's no need to rinse. Only use this on genuine hardwood flooring to bring out the natural grain and luster.

13 SHINE THOSE WINDOWS

Instead of using window-cleaning sprays that contain ammonia, which is harmful to wildlife, wash your windows with pure soap and water and then rinse with a solution of one part vinegar to four parts water. Use washable, reusable cloth instead of paper towels.

14 CLEAN UP WITH VINEGAR

Don't clean your toilet with a mineral-deposits remover as it contains harsh chemicals that harm the environment when flushed down the toilet into the water system. Vinegar is an excellent substitute to scrub off rust and deposits marks.

15 DON'T DISINFECT

For a disinfectant that really works when you absolutely need it (for example, when toilet-training young animals) and also gets rid of grease and even attacks rust, mix 3–6 tablespoons of eucalyptus oil with 2 pints of water and decant into a spray bottle. Shake before use and keep sealed in the refrigerator for up to a month.

16 CLUB STAINS AWAY

To keep fresh stains from sinking deep into clothes, immediately apply a little carbonated water or club soda. The carbonation in the water bubbles up the stain and the salts keep the color from sticking. Then wash as normal.

17 BAKE OFF STAINS

For hard-to-beat, stubborn stains on your kitchen surfaces, dampen a sponge and apply baking powder, then wipe clean as normal. The abrasive powder will get rid of most stains, but if the mark remains, try re-soaking the stain with a solution of baking powder instead.

18 PLANT AWAY SMELLS

Commercial air fresheners work by masking smells and coating the nasal passages with chemicals that diminish the sense of smell by deadening the nerves. In addition, they also pollute the air. Houseplants act as natural air filters, so invest in a few and place them in areas like the kitchen and bathroom where they can counter unpleasant odors.

19 KEEP YOUR HOUSE SMELL-FREE

Use baking soda to stop nasty odors in your refrigerator or garbage can instead of air fresheners that contain chemicals. The baking soda works to neutralize nasty smells without adverse effects. You can also combine it with lemon juice and water and use it as a room spray.

20 REFRESH NATURALLY

Instead of chemical plug-in air fresheners, place a few slices of citrus fruit such as lemon or orange in a saucepan, together with a few cloves. Simmer the mixture gently for an hour or so to refresh the smell of your house.

21 MAKE YOUR OWN POLISH

Most mass-produced polishes contain solvents that are harmful to the environment. Many of them come in aerosol sprays, which are wasteful and contain harmful gases. Make your own polish by melting 2 tablespoons of paraffin wax with 2 pints mineral oil and a few drops of lemon oil, then apply as normal and polish the surface when dry.

22 SOAP IS GOOD FOR YOU

For homemade liquid soap, grate a bar of pure soap (or use soap flakes) and pour into warm water. Heat until dissolved, then cool and store. Use to refill plastic hand-soap bottles in your kitchen and bathroom. The soap should keep indefinitely if kept in an airtight container and it will mean you're not continually buying more plastic.

23 CUT GREASE NATURALLY

If you want to avoid oven cleaners containing harsh chemicals that pollute the air and waterways, but want to remove the extra grease from your oven, add vinegar to your usual dishwashing detergent or soap and wipe on with a clean cloth, rinsing thoroughly.

24 KEEP YOUR COPPER CLEAN

Instead of chemical metal cleaners and polishes, clean copper with lemon juice or vinegar combined with salt, or try white flour to help you get the fingermarks off chrome. For brass, try equal parts of salt and flour on a dry rag, adding a little vinegar if required.

25 STARCH YOUR CARPETS

It is possible to fully clean and deodorize carpets without resorting to chemical-laden carpet cleaners or shampoo. Simply vacuum, liberally sprinkle cornstarch or baking soda, leave one hour, then vacuum again. To remove tough stains, try cold club soda or repeatedly blot with vinegar and soapy water instead of automatically reaching for the stain remover.

26 SWEEP IT AWAY

Try using a broom or a dustpan and brush as a low-energy, environmentally-friendly alternative to vacuuming floors and carpets. Some vacuum cleaners come with reusable dust bags, which you empty and reuse, but even better are those that work without bags.

27 BRUSH UP YOUR SILVER

Use a damp cloth to work white (non-gel) toothpaste into the silver you want to clean, then rinse and dry. The mild abrasive in the toothpaste will clean the silver without resorting to chemical cleaners.

28 KEEP SINKS CLEAR

Your drains can be kept open, clean, and odor-free without the use of corrosive cleaners by simply keeping to two main rules of thumb—never pour liquid grease down a drain and always use a drain strainer to avoid any waste clogging the pipes.

29 DRAIN AWAY DIRT

Use a plumber's auger, known as a "snake" or "toilet jack," for clogged drains before you reach for the abrasive chemicals. Even better, opt for natural acid-alkali cleaning and sprinkle ¼ cup baking soda followed ½ cup vinegar to fizz out accumulated gunk. Flush with boiling water.

30 SOME LIKE IT HOT

You don't need commercial stain remover! For grease stains on white cottons, strain boiling water through the fabric and follow with dry baking soda, or rub with washing soda in water. For other materials, blot the stain with a towel, dampen with water, and rub with soap and baking soda, then wash in hot water.

31 WASH DRAINS THROUGH

Instead of waiting until your drains become blocked and then resorting to harsh drain cleaners, mix 2 tablespoons each of baking soda and salt and pour into the drain, rinsing with boiling water, followed by a quick cold water rinse. Do this once a week as a maintenance measure.

32 MILK AWAY INK

A great way to remove ink stains without polluting the environment by using ammonia-based cleaners is to soak the item in milk, then wash as normal.

33 BE A GOOD CLEANING EGG

To remove coffee and chocolate stains on clothes and kitchen towels, mix egg yolk with lukewarm water and rub onto the stain, then wash as normal.

34 ICE OFF YOUR GUM

Don't resort to expensive and highly chemical solutions for getting rid of chewing gum stuck to clothing. Instead, rub with ice and the gum will slowly flake off.

35 CLEAN CLOTHES WITHOUT BLEACH

If you want to get rid of blood in your clothes without using bleach, pour salt or cold club soda onto the stain and soak in cold water before washing. For a more stubborn stain, mix cornstarch, talcum powder, and a little water into a spreadable paste and apply; then allow to dry and brush away.

36 DON'T THROW RUST AWAY

Instead of throwing away clothes that are damaged by rust marks, saturate the rust stains with sour milk (milk mixed with a little vinegar or lemon juice) and rub the stain with salt. Place the item in direct sunlight until dry, then wash it; the rust stain should have disappeared.

37 DE-SCORCH WITH MILK

To remove iron scorches from colorfast clothing and fabrics, gently simmer the scorched article in 1 cup soap flakes (or grated pure-Castile soap) and 4 pints of milk for 10 minutes. Then rinse thoroughly, allow to dry, and wash normally.

38 POLISH OFF WATERMARKS

Instead of using chemical treatments for wood, or varnishes that contain air-polluting chemicals, get rid of watermarks using a dry cloth. Rub the mark with olive or almond oil, or mix butter with cigarette ash to turn it brown, then polish.

do-it-yourself

39 DON'T VARNISH FLOORS

Instead of varnish that contains chemicals
and can harm wildlife if it finds its way into
the environment, choose natural flaxseed oil
as a sealant for wooden furniture and floors.
It will protect the wood naturally without
you having to worry about fumes.

40 BUY NATURAL PAINT

Synthetic paints can contain fungicides
and heavy metals so the greenest choice
is to buy natural paints instead,
particularly those made from
vegetable or mineral compounds
and which have not undergone
severe production processes.

41 MASK THE SMELL

Make sure you always wear gloves and
a mask when dealing with any kind of
solvent in your home, and also that the
area you are working in is well ventilated.
Solvents can be very dangerous if inhaled.
They can also settle on furnishings and
upholstery, and contribute to the air
pollution in your home.

42 MAKE PLANTS YOUR BASE

Many do-it-yourself companies now
make products based on plant substances
instead of those manufactured by using
dangerous chemicals. Choose plant-based
products wherever possible to limit your
environmental impact.

43 OPEN YOUR DOORS

Even if you have chosen to use natural
paint or varnish in your home rather
than those containing toxic solvents,
make sure you still keep your windows
and doors open to reduce air pollution in
your home. You should wear a mask as
well for extra protection.

44 DISPOSE OF PAINT PROPERLY

Never throw unwanted paint down the sink where it can cause chemicals to build up in waterways. Instead, let it dry and dispose of it at a local government site with specialist paint-disposal or hazardous-waste facilities.

45 DON'T BE A DRIP

Avoid no-drip paints because they may contain polyurethane, which is an environmental hazard. Instead, use a natural fiber brush and apply a little paint at a time to avoid dripping.

46 CHOOSE WATER-BASE FOR WOODWORK

Solvent paints contain more volatile organic compounds and solvents than latex, so for areas that traditionally would have used an oil-based paint, choose one of the new water-based acrylic latex versions instead.

47 CHOOSE SHELLAC

Instead of choosing normal, chemical-ridden paint, try shellac. This is a natural paint that helps walls to breathe, thereby reducing the problem of moisture collection in walls.

48 WASH WITH LIME

Limewash is a good paint alternative for living areas if you can't find mineral- or plant-based paints. It's a more natural product and you'll avoid some of the potentially hazardous chemical compounds in modern paints.

49 BE A WATER BABY

Apart from being bad for the environment, solvent-containing paint strippers could also be carcinogenic. Try water-based alternatives. They might require a little more elbow grease but usually work just as well—without the fumes!

50 CLOSE SHAVE

If you're stripping paint, especially in older homes, make sure you throw your paint shavings away in a sealed container. This stops them giving off lead or toxins, which could be poisonous to humans and wildlife.

51 GIVE BORAX THE THUMBS UP

If you are papering walls and want to stop mold and mildew growing on paper, use borax instead of fungicide (which contains potentially toxic chemicals) in your paste.

52 WOODEN WALLS

If you're choosing wallpaper for your home, try woodchip wallpaper, rice paper, or wood veneer coverings from sustainably managed forests, which uses fewer resources in the production process than vinyl wallpapers.

53 VINYL IS DEAD

Don't cover your floor with vinyl flooring, because it contains PVC, which is manufactured in a way that is very harmful to the environment. Choose linoleum or other natural materials instead.

54 GO FOR SLATE EFFECT

Instead of buying new slates for your roof, why not use slate-effect tiles made from recycled plastic? You won't really notice the difference, except that they'll boost the insulation of your home.

55 TREAD ON WOOD

A wooden floor requires little energy during the manufacturing process and doesn't deplete the world's resources or release toxins. But make sure it is sustainably sourced.

56 INSULATE YOUR FLOOR

To make the most of the heating system in your home, make sure you insulate your floor properly, leaving gaps for ventilation but not enough space for drafts to develop.

57 GET SOFT UNDERFOOT

Wool carpets are a good green choice for floors, but only if they haven't been treated and dyed with toxic chemicals. Choose those dyed with natural colors or vegetable dyes, and avoid chemically treated anti-stain varieties.

58 BACK YOURSELF UP

Check your carpet backing to make sure your floor lives up to its green potential. Woolen felt is the best option because it's stimulating, soft underfoot, environmentally sound and naturally sourced.

59 GET A MINERAL SOLUTION

Instead of lubricants containing solvents, use castor oil and mineral-based lubricants to oil switches and hinges. They are less harmful in manufacture and disposal.

60 STONE COLD

Stone isn't a green a choice for floors because of the high costs involved in transporting it. Salvaged stone is a better alternative because you're reusing old materials, which cuts down environmental costs.

61 SAY NO TO PVC

Everything about the manufacture, distribution and disposal of PVC (polyvinyl chloride) is damaging to the environment and toxic to humans, so avoid using it in your home whenever you can. It is the most common plastic used in building materials and items for the home, such as shower curtains and children's toys. A range of hazardous pollutants and toxins are produced as by-products and it is carcinogenic.

62 PUT A CORK ON IT

Cork is a fantastic choice if you're looking for a green alternative for walls and floors because it's biodegradable, sustainable, and nonpolluting. Cork trees can live 150 years and in addition to producing cork, they also support wildlife in their local habitat.

63 GO NATURAL

For a natural-look floor that's halfway between carpet and wood, choose natural materials like seagrass, coir, sisal, or jute. They are biodegradable and renewable at source. They are also hardwearing, meaning you won't have to replace them regularly.

64 SALVAGE YOUR FLOOR

For flooring, granite and slate are both high-cost in terms of environment because a lot of energy is required to quarry and transport them. Use wood flooring or visit a local salvage yard and try to buy reclaimed granite or slate.

65 TEAK A GOOD LOOK

Make sure you look at labels carefully when buying new outdoor furniture. Avoid those made from teak, mahogany, rosewood, kapur, ebony, or ramin woods. All are threatened hardwood species. Instead, choose 100% recycled teak, recovered by hand from old structures.

66 START A PANEL SHOW

Instead of painting walls, consider wood paneling. Not only is it a good insulator, but it's also really hardwearing, which means you won't have to replace it for many years.

67 LATEX IS GOOD FOR YOU

Choose water-based latex paints over solvent-based paints for your home, and opt for those colored with vegetables rather than fume-releasing chemical compounds.

68 TAKE THE LEAD

Never use lead-based paints. Lead is a toxic substance that can cause changes in brain chemistry and developmental problems. It continues releasing toxins for many years, so if you have an old house, it's also worth checking that you're lead free.

69 AT YOUR DISPOSAL

Never throw toxic household waste that may contain solvents, such as paint thinner and cleaner, in the garbage or sink. Check with your local government facilities for hazardous-waste disposal options.

heating & energy

70 BE A CHIMNEY SWEEP

If you have a solid-fuel fire, keep your chimney clean in order to reduce your dioxide emissions. Clean chimneys involve fewer chemical reactions as the smoke rises, which is healthier for the atmosphere.

71 STORE SOME HEAT

If you have a wood-burning stove or a wood fire, makes sure it is EPA-certified and think about incorporating a heat storage system which could put the energy it produces to some use—such as heating water or walls— rather than it being wasted up the chimney.

72 SUSTAIN YOUR WOOD

Buy wood to use as fuel from sustainable sources like managed forestry systems and local wood suppliers. It's better for the environment to use wood that has been transported shorter distances and that hasn't contributed to deforestation.

73 NO SMOKE WITHOUT FIRE

Open-log fires waste 85% of the fuel they burn and use 15 times the volume of air in the room for every hour they burn, compensating by sucking air into the room and causing draughts. Wood-burning or wood-pellet stoves are much more energy-efficient choices.

74 DON'T WASTE WOOD

Storage and reuse of recovered wood waste are often problematic, so ask your local government if you are able to buy it from them to use as cheap firewood.

75 BE A SCRAP BURNER

Local tree surgeons and construction companies sometimes sell off their wood waste and cuttings cheaply. You can use this at home as fuel for wood fires. Choose a company that is as local as possible to cut down on transportation costs.

76 BRICK IT UP

Where you can, choose solid masonry for your fireplace and chimney as it is one of the best materials for holding onto heat for longer and preventing energy wastage.

77 BURN IT DRY

If you have a fireplace or wood-burning stove at home, make sure your wood is mature and dry. Burning green or damp wood releases carcinogens into the atmosphere, contributing to air pollution and acid rain.

78 TILE YOURSELF OUT

The most energy-efficient choice for fireplaces is to choose a wood-burning, heat-storing tile stove, which has the highest energy efficiency rating of any burner fire. Replacing your existing open fire with one of these could halve your energy wastage.

79 LIGHT YOUR FIRE

Use twigs and paper to start fires rather than firestarters, whether it's the barbecue, your wood-burning stove or an open fire indoors or out. Firestarters and fire-lighting liquids are made using chemicals which can be highly toxic.

80 GET SMOKE-FREE

Instead of polluting the atmosphere every time you light up your fire or grill with wood or charcoal, think about using smoke-free fuel, especially in residential areas.

81 LEAVE IT AJAR

If you have a solid-fuel fire, make sure you don't exclude all the drafts from your room. Leave a door slightly open as a fire requires some circulating air in order for it to burn most efficiently.

82 RAD UP YOUR RADS

Place radiators on internal rather than external walls. In this position, the radiation will be most efficient, as the walls will naturally hold some of the heat and heat loss is diminished.

83 DRAW AT DUSK

At dusk when the air outside begins to cool down, your home is susceptible to losing more heat. Draw your drapes and shades at dusk, before it gets completely dark, to help conserve energy.

84 REPLACE FILTERS REGULARLY

If you have a stove, heater, or furnace that uses filters, replace them regularly because they use more energy when they're full of dust. Even better, choose washable versions and make sure they're cleaned once a month.

85 DON'T GO ELECTRIC

Electric heating loses 90% of its energy due to inefficient transmission through the grid system and through electrical appliances that aren't as energy efficient as they could be. Try switching to other, more efficient, energy sources.

86 GET IN CONTROL

Fit thermostatic radiator valves to radiators in every room to avoid wasting energy by heating some rooms more than you need to. This will enable you to control the temperature of each room without affecting the others, thereby only heating what you need. Keep bedrooms cooler than the rest of the house and don't waste heat on communal areas like hallways and stairs.

87 FOIL A PLAN

Don't throw away your aluminum foil. Place a sheet behind radiators with the shiny side facing the room. Because of the reflective properties of the metal, heat will be radiated back into the room, making your heating system more efficient.

88 GET A COLD ROOM

Don't waste energy by heating your whole house if you're not using all the rooms. Turn radiators off in guest rooms or an office that is not in daily use, and turn them on only when you're actually occupying the rooms.

89 GO THERMOSTATIC

You don't have to invest in a whole new heating system to make your house more energy efficient. Simply add new controls to your existing heating system, such as a thermostat in a central area, to stop your home heating up more than necessary.

90 SHELVE THE HEAT

Instead of leaving a huge space above your radiator, try putting up a shelf a few feet above it to trap some of the heat released by the top of the radiator and keep the room hotter.

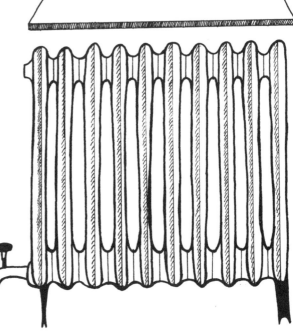

91 WARM UP WITH WOOL

Use natural materials like wood and fabric in your home to keep it warm during winter. Hard, manmade substances don't hold onto heat and therefore require more heating to maintain a warm temperature. Go natural whenever you can.

92 PUT A CORK IN HEAT LOSS

To help improve the heat balance in your living room, use natural fabrics like cork and wood wherever you can. These materials retain heat in the winter, keeping the room warm, but also keep rooms cool during the summer months.

93 GET WITH THE PROGRAM

Instead of a heating timer for your central heating, install a programable thermostat so the heating will only be used when it's really needed, minimizing heat wastage and fuel consumption. If you are out at an office all day long, there's no need to heat your home. Make sure the thermostat is in the middle of the house and not near a door.

94 ADD A LAYER

Before cranking up the heating, try putting on a sweater and socks. Adding an extra layer rather than turning up your heating is the easiest way to save heating costs—both on your pocket and the environment.

95 FLUSH YOUR SYSTEM

If your radiators are warm at the top but not at the bottom, you've probably got debris build-up. Instead of installing a whole new heating system, consider having your radiators flushed through to remove debris and boost efficiency.

96 BLEED IT OUT

If your radiators are warm at the bottom but not at the top, particularly at the top of the house, you probably need to bleed the air from your system. Most systems function more efficiently if this is done at least once a month to keep the system totally air free.

97 LEAVE IT LOW

If you go on a winter vacation, make sure you leave your heating on the lowest level, and use a timer switch on the thermostat. The heating only needs to be on for a short time every day to prevent pipes from freezing—while you're away your aim should be to prevent freezing, not to actually heat the rooms.

98 ONE DEGREE COOLER

Turning your heating system down 5–10 degrees could save you 5–10% on heating bills. You'll probably not even notice the difference in temperature, but you're sure to notice the saving on your utility bill. Reduce the heat just one degree at a time and try it for a week to see how you go.

99 COOL DOWN YOUR WATER

Most people keep their hot water at much too hot a temperature and need cold water to cool it down, wasting precious heat energy. Turn your water heater down to 130°F—at this temperature the water is hot enough to kill bacteria but "cool" enough to save energy.

100 TURN IT ON

It might not sound very green, but leaving your heating on constantly for a few days (not nights) at the beginning of the heating season might actually save you energy in the long run. It allows the walls and floors to heat up fully, which means you'll need less energy to maintain heat later.

101 DON'T RUN ON EMPTY

Don't waste energy by heating an empty house, even for short periods. When you go out for an evening in the winter, either turn off your heating completely or set the timer to switch on half an hour before you plan to arrive home.

102 HOTTY BOTTY

Instead of an electric blanket, take a hot water bottle to bed to keep your feet warm. Or wear a pair of bedsocks, which will keep you warm all night without using any extra energy.

103 BE A FAN

Ceiling fans can reduce air conditioning costs by as much as 40% in the summer. Amazingly, they can also save energy in winter! By agitating the air and stopping cool air from pooling at ground level, they can reduce heating bills by 10%.

104 CONDENSE YOUR HEAT

Condensing furnaces or boilers are the most efficient, with 88% of fuel converted into heat compared to 72% with conventional versions. However, the water vapors the boilers let off can be irritating so make sure you site your flue away from your neighbors' windows and patios. Consider choosing a condenser if you need to replace an existing gas or oil central-heating furnace.

105 GET TANKED UP

If your water heater is more than five years old and has no internal insulation, you are most probably losing vital heat through lack of insulation. Invest in an insulating jacket for your tank and watch your energy use fall.

106 MAKE YOURSELF A LOG

Instead of throwing away your old newspaper, invest in a log-making machine that compresses and moistens old newspapers and makes them into slow-burning logs for your fire or wood-burning stove.

107 PAPER YOUR FLOOR

For extra insulation, lay newspaper under your carpet underlay. Choose a good-quality underlay that is thick and foamy to the touch, and it will hold the heat in better.

108 CLOSE YOUR DOORS

Remember to close doors behind you when entering or leaving rooms. Many people don't realize that shutting doors, especially if they lead onto a hallway or to the outside, helps conserve a lot of heat by cutting down on drafts.

109 PIPE DREAMS

Insulate your electric hot water heater and hot water pipes to prevent heat wastage. Start with the pipe insulation material, or pipe lagging, 6 inches from the heater. (Gas heaters should not be insulated, because of the possible build-up of gas.)

110 BE A COPPER TOP

If you are installing solar panels, make sure you have copper pipes. Copper has higher conductivity than other metals, so it will make your solar system more efficient by cutting down on heat wastage.

111 DRAW THE DRAPES

To help preserve heat on winter evenings, cover windows or French doors with heavy, floor-length curtains to help reduce drafts and so conserve heat in the room. In very cold houses it is a good idea to hang heavy drapes over doors and doorways, too.

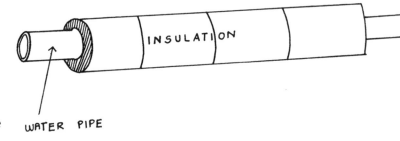

INSULATION

WATER PIPE

112 FILL YOUR GAPS

Fill in the gaps between your floor and
baseboards to avoid drafts that might reduce
the temperature, forcing you to rely more on
heating. Fitting wall-to-wall carpets will have
the same effect.

113 CHECK YOUR INSULATION

Invest in an insulation check by an
expert, who will advise you where you
can make energy savings in your home
simply by adding insulation materials.
You'll soon recoup the cost of the expert
in energy savings.

114 DRAFT A PLAN

To prevent drafts coming in through external
doors, buy or sew a fabric batting-stuffed
draft stopper that lies across the bottom
of the doorframe and prevents wind from
coming in underneath.

home design

115 CONSERVE YOUR SUN

Add a sunroom to your home to trap the heat of the sun and cut your heating bills. But make sure you have firmly closing doors between the sunroom and the main part of your house. If you don't, heat will be sucked from your home on gloomy days.

116 PLAY ECO-HOUSE

Eco houses made from old car and tractor tires are now available in ready-to-build kits so you can build your own totally green house to live in. They are energy- and resource-efficient, and have inventive designs. Or if you're really serious, join some like minds and build a home in one of the growing number of sustainable communities and eco-villages worldwide, such as Arcosanti in Arizona.

117 BE A WATER REED

If you have enough land attached to your home, install a totally natural reed-bed sewage system. It will naturally decompose your waste and minimize the effect you have on the environment by cutting water pollution.

118 MAKE HAY WHILE THE SUN SHINES

Think creatively about the substances you use for insulation. Hay and straw bales are fantastic insulation and, if they are packed properly, can also help to prevent fire from spreading (see www.thelaststraw.org).

119 GET HIGH SPEC

For exterior windows, doors, and skylights, choose the highest specification glass you can because it will help insulate your house. Or consider replacing old doors and windows with a higher spec alternative.

120 RAM YOUR RUBBLE

Recycle bricks by passing them onto salvage yards or donating them to local construction workers. If you're having building work done, use the bricks as rammed rubble to help strengthen and insulate walls.

121 LIVE OFF THE EARTH

Several companies now manufacture plaster made from earth, so it has little cost to the environment and is biodegradable. A substitute for gypsum plaster and paint, earth plaster is a nontoxic combination of clays, aggregates, and natural pigments.

122 ADOBE YOUR WALLS

Choose interior adobe walls for your home to increase your thermal mass and reduce heat loss, thereby cutting energy usage.

123 SEARCH FOR SUNLIGHT

In order to avoid relying on electric lights unnecessarily, try to arrange your space around the way light falls naturally. In the northern hemisphere, south-facing portions have the most available light (or north-facing in the southern hemisphere), so think about making these the rooms you use the most.

124 WOOD IS GOOD

For the sun-facing parts of your house, choose wooden floors since they make the most of the warmth they get from the sun. They hold onto the warmth for longer, meaning you're wasting less energy. But make sure you don't have gaps between floorboards that can cause drafts.

125 GET OUT OF THE SHADOWS

Help your house heat up naturally in the sunshine by avoiding planting trees that will overshadow it, especially on the sunny side of the house. Know the full height the tree will grow to before committing to a position. This will help reduce your heating bills and your impact on the environment.

126 IN THE HOT WATER

Solar hot water heaters are becoming much more common as technology makes them more efficient and less bulky. Solar power is a great way to heat water in your home, via copper pipes that transfer heat quickly.

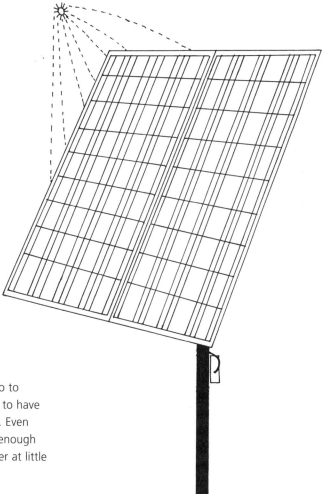

127 SUNNY SIDE UP

When house hunting or looking for a site to build your new home, remember that it should face the sunny aspect and be sheltered from the prevailing cold winds. This will make considerable savings on your heating bill.

128 GO SOLAR

One of the best things you can do to help save energy in your house is to have solar panels installed in your roof. Even the murkiest winter climates get enough sunshine to produce electric power at little extra cost to the environment.

129 DO A HEADSTAND

It might sound a strange way to live, but in a two-story house it actually makes more environmental sense to have your bedrooms downstairs and your living space at the top of the house because heat rises, and you are likely to want your living space to be warmer than your bedrooms.

130 GET GRAPHIC

Metal-and-glass structures make great additions to modern buildings because they encourage the best use of light and are very long lasting, unlike old-fashioned wood-and-glass structures. Choose them for sunrooms, conservatories, and extensions.

131 SEE DOUBLE

Always choose double glazing for windows. The layer of air trapped inside the glass prevents heat loss into the cold outdoors and will insulate your house against heat loss in winter. Similarly, it will keep you cooler in summer. The optimum space between the two panes is ¾ inch. A smaller one leads to greater heat loss.

132 THINK FOR THE FUTURE

If you're building a house or making home improvements, think about the future as well as your current needs. Try to make changes in such a way that other people can add to them in the future without having to tear the whole thing down and start again.

133 SAY "TIMBER"

Make sure your external glazed doors have wide timber frames, reducing the glazing area that could contribute to heat loss, but retaining the perception of large openings and lots of light.

134 BUILD WITH BAMBOO

Use bamboo plywood for your joinery projects—sustainably harvested and totally renewable, it cuts, stains, and routers just like ordinary plywood but is stiffer and much stronger. It is mostly left untreated but can can be treated with an oil-based finish. You can also get premade bamboo countertops, paneling and furniture that is laminated with a non-toxic formaldehyde-free adhesive.

home habits

135 GIVE NOTICE

In many areas, free local papers are delivered as a standard service. Write to your local paper provider or leave a note asking for no free local paper if you don't read it. If you do read it, make sure you recycle it or use it as dry material in your compost.

136 JUNK THE JUNK

Be honest—how many of those brochures and leaflets that fill up your mailbox do you actually read? Thousands of leaflets are thrown away each year, contributing to paper waste. Try putting a notice on your door or mailbox saying "no junk mail."

137 EDIT THE NEWS

Cut down on the number of newspapers you buy. Attempt to limit yourself to one per household, but if you do want two, alternate days instead of buying both every day. Many coffee shops have areas where you can leave your paper for others to read. Alternatively, read your paper online.

138 OPT OUT

Check whether your local government has a state-registered opt-out schemes for junk mail. You put your name and address on a list to ensure you don't receive unwanted mail through your mailbox and so reduce your paper waste.

139 THINK INNOVATION

When it comes to furnishing your home, look for modern green materials wherever possible—such as the rugs and insulation materials made from recycled drink cartons that are now coming onto the market. Also look for green alternatives for floors and upholstery material. There are many plastics available made from recycled goods that can be used for kitchen surfaces or flooring, too.

140 DUST OFF APPLIANCES

Invest in a dust cover to cover any electrical equipment, such as televisions, DVD players, and computers. This prevents dust from being taken into the air vents and reducing performance, which, in turn, makes them less energy efficient.

141 BUY SECONDHAND

Instead of always buying new items for your home, think about visiting flea markets, secondhand stores, and garage sales. You may pick up a few bargains and at the same time contribute to reducing waste.

142 PAPER YOUR LAMPS

Choose paper lampshades rather than plastic because they are much easier to manufacture and dispose of. They are also available in many different colors to complement your room scheme. Choose those with metal or wood bindings, rather than plastic.

143 CHOOSE TO REUSE

Wherever you can, avoid single-use products that you will have to dispose of after use. Instead, choose items that will last for longer and can be reused or refilled. As a general rule, the more plastic they contain, the more you should try and reuse.

144 BAMBOO YOUR HOME

Choose bamboo for window shades and flooring. It is a great green choice for your home because it grows incredibly fast— some species up to 3 feet a day—and doesn't need pesticides or fertilizers. One of the hardest natural materials, it is an excellent substitute for hardwood and a sustainable resource.

145 GET WATER-POWERED

Always keep an eye on new inventions. On the market is a new water-based battery you simply have to fill up with water every few months to keep it working. Ultimately you may be able to choose these instead of relying on traditional alkaline batteries for such products as clocks and calculators.

146 DON'T BE LEAD ASTRAY

Choose candles without a lead wick. During manufacture lead wicks may leak heavy metal ions into natural surroundings. Test for this by dragging paper across the wick—if it leaves a mark, it contains lead.

147 GET NATURAL UNDERFOOT

Reduce the levels of pollution inside your own home by choosing carpet made from natural rather than synthetic fibers. Synthetics release toxins and air pollutants that could be inhaled by you and your family. In addition, older carpets can contain chemicals that have since been banned and can also have a build-up of toxins such as cigarette smoke or pesticides.

148 LOOK AFTER YOUR BUTT

It is estimated that a third of all smoked cigarettes end up as litter. Make sure that your cigarette has been put out properly and you dispose of the butt in a waste can or designated area.

149 LIMIT YOUR ELECTRICS

Try to limit the amount of electromagnetic equipment in each room in your house. Electromagnetic equipment emits radiation, which is believed to be harmful to health. It also causes static build-up. Aim for no more than one or two electrical items per room.

150 GET SOME WALL MATERIAL

By choosing a burlap-based wallpaper for your walls you will reduce your noise pollution by trapping sound as well as help insulate your room, meaning you'll use less energy to keep it warm. Other eco-friendly wallcoverings that are natural, renewable, and recyclable include grasscloth, sisal, and silk. Look for those made with water-based inks.

151 HANG THE HEATING

As an alternative to painting walls or putting up wallpaper, think about hanging natural fabric wall hangings to insulate the walls and help trap warmth inside.

152 DUST UP A STORM

Instead of throwing away old T-shirts and letting the material go to waste, tear them up and use instead of store-bought dusters. You'll have a never-ending supply of rags for cleaning and wiping up, and they can simply be washed and reused time and time again!

153 UNPLUG YOUR CHARGER

It takes a forest with an area equivalent to 500 soccer fields to absorb all the carbon dioxide produced by cell phone chargers that are left plugged into electrical outlets. Make sure you unplug your charger when the battery is full. Or alternatively choose an Energy-Star charger; according to the EPA, if every phone sold annually in the U.S. used an Energy Star charger, the energy saved could light 760,000 homes for a year.

154 BOTTLE YOUR IDEAS

Before you send your plastic bottles for recycling, think of ways you can use them in your home that will prevent you from having to buy more plastic. For example, cutting the ends off water bottles turns them into excellent protective covers for seedlings in the garden.

155 CREATE A THROUGH-DRAFT

If your house gets too hot in the summer, plan to open selective windows and doors to create a through-draft—for example, opening the front and the back doors can be an efficient way to keep the house cool. This will help keep it cool inside even when it's hot outside. It's even worth building a new window into a room, but make sure it's double glazed.

156 FILTER OUT THE JUNK

Keep your home air and filter systems fine-tuned by regular servicing and washing or changing filters regularly. That way, they'll use the minimum amount of energy required to function properly.

157 WELCOME THE WIND

Many products can cause air pollution to build up in your home, including modern cleaners, which contain strong chemicals. Make sure you ventilate your home well, ensuring a through-flow of air to help reduce pollution levels and encourage good ventilation.

158 BRUSH IT UP

Don't throw away your old toothbrush; use it to clean tricky-to-reach areas like the caulking between floor and wall tiles and the area around bathroom faucets. Often a little more elbow grease will do the trick without resorting to harsh cleaners.

159 FILTER IT AWAY

The human body requires at least 1 gallon of water a day. If you are considering stocking up on emergency supplies, bear in mind that plastic bottles are thought to leach chemicals into the water if left for a length of time. Save space and the environment by stocking up on water filters instead.

160 LIGHT IT UP

Most people keep a flashlight in their homes in case of emergency. Make yours a green version by choosing one that recharges through cranking or shaking rather than a battery-operated one.

161 BUY RECYCLED

Always buy recycled garbage bags, made from a variety of reused plastics. They are available from most supermarkets and hardware stores. There's no difference in quality and you'll be making your garbage that little bit greener.

162 HUNT THE MERCURY

Inventory your house for products containing mercury, which can be found in a wide variety of household products, including paint, thermometers, batteries, fluorescent lights, and disinfectants. Mercury is easily absorbed through the skin and respiratory system and exposure can cause brain and liver damage. If, for example, your fever thermometer has a mercury filling, carefully dispose of it as hazardous waste and buy a safer digital thermometer.

163 AUDIT YOUR FOOTPRINT

If you're worried about your impact on the environment, hire an environmental auditor to assess your "carbon footprint." (see www. carbonfootprint.com) and find out how you can make changes. Many companies now have specialists who will visit your home.

164 LIGHTS OUT

Instead of leaving your house lights on when you go on vacation, install a timer or remote-controlled lighting system so you can use them as little as possible.

165 DON'T THROW THE SACK

An astounding 30% of landfills in the U.S. are devoted to black garbage bags. Set up your own reusing scheme for garbage bags by transferring your trash to a single outdoor receptacle and reusing the bags in the inside trash cans whenever you can.

166 TURN IT OFF

Turn off your refrigerator and leave the door open when you go on vacation—what's the point of wasting energy to keep nothing cool for the whole time you're away? If you don't have an automatic defrosting unit, defrost regularly in order to keep the fridge at its maximum cooling ability and avoid running the fridge or freezer at colder temperatures than necessary.

167 BE A DAY BUG

Daylight is the highest quality lighting and it's free! Locate your work surfaces, reading spots, and important areas near windows or skylights and you won't need to use artificial lighting during the day, saving precious energy.

indoor pests

168 NO MORE ANTS

To get rid of ants without resorting to chemicals, locate the entrance to the nest, squeeze a lemon onto it, and leave the peel. Ants will also retreat from lines of talcum powder, chalk, bone meal, charcoal dust, and cayenne pepper.

169 SUGAR AWAY INSECTS

Don't use poisonous insecticide powders to kill cockroaches and ants—these might enter the food chain and poison other wildlife, too. Borax mixed with confectioner's sugar will kill them, but is harmless to other animals.

170 ANTS IN YOUR PANTS

Common household pesticides can easily find their way into local water sources, sometimes at levels that can harm aquatic life. Don't sprinkle toxic ant powder in your cupboards—hang sage and pennyroyal instead to deter ants—they hate the smell and will leave your food alone.

171 PLUG AWAY COCKROACHES

To get rid of cockroaches without poison, plug all small cracks along baseboards, wall shelves, cupboards, and around pipes, sinks, and bathtub fixtures. For a trap, you can try lightly greasing the inner neck of a small glass bottle and putting a little stale beer or a raw potato in the bottom.

172 CLOSE YOUR WINDOWS

A sunny window is the most common entrance for flies, so close open windows before the sun hits them during the day. If you stop flies from entering your home in the first place, you won't be tempted to use aerosol insecticides to get rid of them.

173 POT YOUR MINT

The potent chemical compounds in pesticides are much more harmful to the environment and to you than the insects themselves. For a natural deterrent, if you want your windows open but don't want them to be an invitation to flying pests, grow mint in pots around windows. Because mint is a natural insect repellent, this will keep them from entering.

174 GET RID OF FLIES

Instead of using poisonous aerosol fly spray, make a package of cloves, eucalyptus, and peppermint to hang in kitchen cupboards and drawers as deterrent.

175 TRAP FRUIT FLIES

For a natural way to trap annoying fruit flies, pour a small amount of beer into a wide-mouthed jar to attract them. Use a rubber band to secure a plastic bag across the mouth of the jar and poke a small hole in the bag. Flies will enter through the hole and not be able to find their way out again.

176 MAKE SOME FLYPAPER

Use regular sticky flypaper to catch unwelcome flying guests, or better still, make your own by dipping yellow paper into honey. Hang up with a saucer below to catch the excess drip. It may seem a bit messy but it's very effective and all-natural.

177 REPEL MOTHS NATURALLY

Moth-proof your clothes using a mixture of lavender oil and cedarwood oil, which are natural moth repellents. Commercial moth repellents usually contain para-dichlorobenzene, a carcinogenic toxic. Very high usage of p-DCB products in the home can result in dizziness, headaches, and liver problems.

178 DON'T SHUT YOUR TRAP

If you leave rat poison in your kitchen or roof space, you can't control the amount of poison they ingest. You will also run the risk of harm to domestic pets or family members who may encounter the poison. Traps are a much greener way to get rid of them. Alternatively, choose a pest removal company that employs humane, nontoxic methods.

179 NO MORE MOTHS

To trap moths, mix one part sugar syrup with two parts vinegar and place it in a margarine or yogurt container. Clean it regularly. Cedar chips or black pepper also works well as all-natural moth deterrents—use them in cloth bags placed in drawers or hung in closets.

180 TRAP SILVERFISH

To trap silverfish, mix up one part molasses to two parts vinegar. Place the mixture near cracks and holes where pests live. Silverfish can also be repelled by treating table legs and cracks in cupboards with a mixture of borax and honey.

181 LEARN TO LIVE WITH SPIDERS

Spiders are great for pest control because of the large number of insects they prey on, including a number of pest species. If you can leave them alone to peacefully coexist with you in your home, they will help you by catching insects that infest houseplants as well as flies. If they live by windows, they will prevent pests from entering.

182 GET HOT WITH PESTS

Instead of using pesticides for houseplants, blend two or three very hot chili peppers, half an onion and a clove of garlic in water, boil, then allow to cool and transfer to a sealed container. Steep for two days and strain. Used as a spray, this liquid is good for indoor and outdoor plants and can be frozen for future use.

183 BAY AWAY WEEVILS

Steer clear of insecticides that can leak poisons into the food chain. As a harmless way to keep weevils out of your flour, rice, and legumes, simply add dried bay leaves to the containers in which you store them.

184 WASH AWAY FLEAS

If your pets are infested with ticks or fleas, prepare a herbal rinse by steeping rosemary in boiling water and allowing it to cool. Wash the pet well with soap and warm water, dry thoroughly, then apply the rinse. Do not towel down your pet, as this will remove the residue, but make sure your pet is dry before letting him out.

185 BURN AWAY MOZZIES

Instead of smothering yourself in chemical mosquito repellents or worse using electric mosquito repellent, burn citronella candles or use citronella oil to stop mosquitos in their tracks. The oils from the citronella plant are used to make topical lotions and sprays but choose a brand without extra additives.

186 PEPPER YOUR WEEVILS

Beans and grains are weevil favorites. To keep the pests away, hang small cloth sacks containing black pepper in your food containers or storage cupboards. Alternatively, add soapnuts (also called soapberries) to cupboards because weevils hate the smell.

187 KEEP CLOTHES CLEAN

Moths are attracted to body oils on clothing, so keep vulnerable clothes clean, dry, and well aired to avoid attack. Camphor can be used because it is the major nontoxic ingredient in mothballs.

188 GET MINTED

Peppermint oil is an excellent deterrent of rats and mice. Sprinkle your attic and cupboards regularly with peppermint spirit or oil to keep them away.

utilities

189 DON'T WASTE ENERGY

Wherever you can, opt for energy produced in sustainable ways. Do some research: Many states run "waste to energy" schemes for converting waste to energy in power stations attached to waste plants.

190 STOP THE DRIP

Just one leaky faucet that drips every three seconds can waste more than 30 gallons of water a month. Get your faucets checked and fix any leaks and drips.

191 CATCH SOME RAYS

Avoid using drapes or sheer curtains on windows that are blessed with full sun. The curtains can block the warming rays of the sun, which in turn can help heat up your home and so cut down on utility bills. Make use of the free energy directly from nature!

192 PULL THE PLUG

LCD displays, battery chargers, remote controls, and many other electrical goods keep on using electricity unless they are unplugged. At least 5% of electricity is consumed by appliances while they are switched off—so be sure to unplug them or press the "off" button when not in use.

193 MULTITASK YOUR HOME

In order to limit the amount of electricity you use, cut down on electromagnetic radiation in your home and reduce your reliance on plastic, choose electrical equipment that performs more than one purpose. A good example of a multitasking product is to buy a combined TV and DVD, rather than two separate machines.

194 CHANGE YOUR BULBS

If every household in the U.S. replaced its next burned-out light bulb with a compact fluorescent bulb, it would save the same amount of carbon dioxide as taking 1.2 million cars off the road for an entire year. Fluorescent bulbs last six to ten times longer than standard incandescent versions and use 75% less energy because they use less heat than standard bulbs.

195 GET A BETTER BULB

For lights that are turned on and off a lot, compact fluorescent bulbs aren't always the best choice because the constant switching on and off can lower their efficiency and burn them out. A low wattage normal incandescent bulb will be more efficient in these areas.

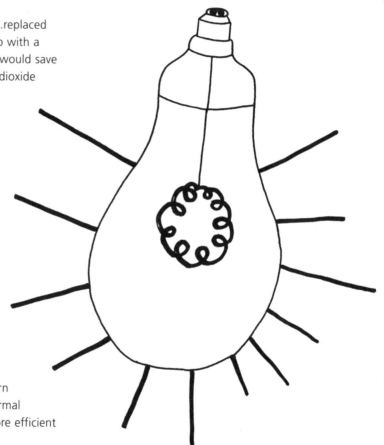

196 TURN IT OFF

To save electricity, always turn off the lights when you leave the room, no matter how long you're leaving for.

197 GET A COMBI

Change your boiler for a combination boiler, avoiding the need for a hot water tank. This way you won't be wasting energy by heating water you might not use, and it will be cheaper, too.

198 WEATHERPROOF WALLS

To stop air leakage from your home, which can reduce the efficiency of your heating system, make sure your walls are weatherproofed. Stripping and caulking surfaces, especially around windows and doors, can help make sure they're water- and wind-tight.

199 DO A STRIP

The most efficient lighting is fluorescent strip lighting, so make sure you use this wherever you can in your home. It's particularly suited to kitchens and bathrooms.

200 SAY HELLO TO HALOGEN

Halogen bulbs last eight times longer than normal bulbs, so choose them wherever you can for energy-efficient lighting. They're great choices for bedside lights and for mood lighting in your living space, but not so good for kitchens or home office areas where you need stronger light for tasks.

201 INSULATE YOUR ROOF

A simple step like insulating your roof could lead to considerable savings on fuel bills because your house will hold onto heat better and require less heating. Choose green insulating materials like recycled paper insulation or natural fabrics like wool.

202 GET AN AUDIT

If you're unsure about how to improve your home's energy efficiency, ask your utility company for a home energy audit. Many of these companies offer them free and they could help you pinpoint energy wastage in your home and recommend solutions.

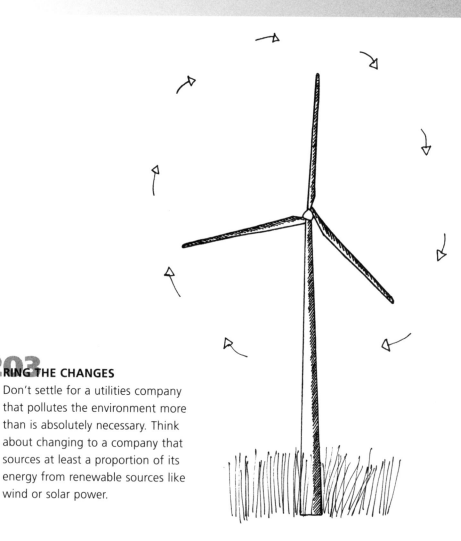

203 RING THE CHANGES

Don't settle for a utilities company
that pollutes the environment more
than is absolutely necessary. Think
about changing to a company that
sources at least a proportion of its
energy from renewable sources like
wind or solar power.

washing & drying

204 BE A SURFACTANT FINDER

Try to steer clear of washing powder containing surfactants (APEs and LAS). They are slow to biodegrade, can damage plants and animals, and are even thought to have an effect on male sex cells in some wild animals.

205 DON'T BE BLOOMY

Many laundry powders contain phosphates and phosphonates. If they find their way into waterways through the drain system, they can cause algal blooms that can suffocate lakes and streams, killing wildlife. Try to choose phosphate-free powders.

206 LOATHSOME LIQUIDS

When it comes to laundry and dishwasher detergents, liquid versions can contain twice as many harmful components, so choose powder or tablets wherever you can to minimize environmental effects.

207 DON'T FILL UP

Laundry powders have, in the past, contained a high level of filling agents that are specially designed so they take up more space. Opt for the latest concentrated powders that don't have as much packaging and also take less energy to transport.

208 CHOOSE VEGETABLE NOT PETROS

Most detergents contain some kind of surfactant (a substance that allows them to foam or penetrate solids), but you can minimize the damage they do to the environment by making sure your surfactants are vegetable-based rather than petrochemical. Choose vegetable-based, naturally derived, or eco-friendly detergents.

209 GET ON YOUR SOAP BOX

Soap is a completely biodegradable product, so making a point of selecting soap-based products wherever you can is always going to be a good green choice. This is particularly important when looking at water-using appliances such as washing machines and dishwashers.

210 BE A BORAX BORE

Borax can be used instead of harsh stain removers to treat blood, chocolate, coffee, and urine as well as mildew stains. If the latter get into water systems, they cause damage to delicate forms of wildlife.

211 WATER AWAY WINE STAINS

To get rid of fruit and wine stains, immediately pour salt or cold club soda directly onto the stain and then soak the stain in milk before washing. In general, it is a good idea to keep a bottle of club soda in the refrigerator for an instant stain remover.

212 DO A SODA SOAK

If you have heavily soiled clothes or whites to wash, instead of simply adding more detergent to your washing machine or using a higher temperature washing cycle, thus using more energy to heat the water, try presoaking your clothes in a solution of baking soda. This will yield the same results, with much less energy wastage and water pollution.

213 CUT DETERGENT IN HALF

Most people tend to use twice as much detergent as necessary to get clothes clean. Instead, try cutting down by half the amount of detergent you use to achieve exactly the same results.

214 WEAR IT MORE THAN ONCE

Instead of indiscriminately throwing everything you've worn into the laundry hamper, make a point of only washing clothes that really need it. Outer layers of clothing such as shirts, sweaters, and pants can be worn more than once without laundering, saving both water and electricity.

215 DONUT ANYONE?

There are a number of devices on the market that will help you to cut down on the amount of laundry detergent you use. One of these is a neat donut-shaped ring that rubs against clothes throughout the wash cycle and so helps your machine to wash everything more deeply while using less detergent.

216 GET MAGNETIC

Wash your clothes the magnetic way without detergent by investing in a unique magnetic washing ball. When agitated, the ball produces ionized oxygen, which reduces the surface tension of water and so allows it to penetrate fabrics and release dirt.

217 SOFTEN NATURALLY

Instead of buying fabric softeners, which can leave chemical residues on clothes and pollute the environment during the manufacturing process, try adding ¼ cup white vinegar to the rinse cycle.

218 DON'T BE A SOFTIE

If it's the beautiful fragrance in fabric softeners that you're really after, simply substitute a few drops of your favorite essential oil instead.

219 FILL IT UP

The average family uses their washing machine five times a week, which means more than 6,000 gallons of water goes through the machine every year. Making sure that you always run full loads will help reduce water wastage and save energy, too.

220 SOAK YOUR SILKS

To clean silk, you don't really need to use your machine's silk cycle or you could end up running an almost empty machine. Instead, soak in approximately 1 cup pure soap mixed with 2–3 tablespoons baking soda, then squeeze the garment gently, rinse well and roll up in a towel to remove excess water.

221 DON'T BLEACH OUT

It's best to avoid harsh bleaches altogether, but if you really prefer to use them in your home, opt for the chlorine-free varieties such as sodium percarbonate, which will cause far less damage to the environment.

222 LOVELY LEMON

Don't use chemically based stain removers on vegetable and fruit stains. Instead, apply lemon juice, a powerful but natural bleaching agent, to get rid of stains before you wash as normal. If you can, dry on a line outdoors in direct sunlight for extra stain-removing power.

223 BOIL YOUR SOCKS

What if you don't want to use bleach but you really can't stand your dirty white socks? Don't worry—simply boil them for five minutes with a slice of lemon and dry on a clothesline for fantastic nonchemical, whiter-than-white results.

224 GO NATURAL FOR STAIN REMOVAL

Instead of using bleach to remove food stains, try a natural solution instead. Add ½ cup of washing soda to each wash load to whiten up your whites and brighten colors. Or add lemon juice to the rinse cycle and then hang your clothes on a clothesline outside in the sun, where the rays will bleach them naturally.

225 GIVE HOT WASHES THE COLD SHOULDER

Try washing your laundry in cold or warm water instead of hot. Studies have shown that clothes get just as clean, and far less energy is used—up to 90% of the energy taken up with washing clothes is used to heat the water.

226 COLD SPLASH

If you choose a cold rinse cycle instead of rinsing with hot water, you'll save electricity every time you wash.

227 DON'T DYE TRYING

Did you know that simply dying clothes can account for most of the water used in their production? Apparently unfixed dye often washes out of garments and can end up polluting rivers with heavy metal fixatives, since treatment plants fail to remove them from the water. Wherever possible, choose natural colors for clothing.

228 STEEL YOURSELF

Almost all of your washing machine can be recycled, so when you invest in a new one, don't just throw the old one away— send the steel to a recycling depot to help reduce landfill.

229 TAKE A WOODEN LINE

For eco-friendly outdoor clothes' drying, make sure you use wooden clothespins and not plastic ones.

230 CHECK YOUR VALVES

If you've had your washing machine or dishwasher for more than five years, get a plumber to check your fittings and valves for leakage and to ensure you're not wasting water. Clear blockages regularly.

231 HANG IT ALL

If you live in an apartment building, buy a wooden clothes rack and hang your clothes on a balcony or in front of an open window.

232 GET RADICAL

It uses more energy to dry clothes than wash them, so instead of tumble-drying, drape wet clothes over radiators or towel warmers. Not only will this save energy, but keeping rooms humid will give your immune system a boost.

233 COVER IT UP

Take a reusable garment bag to the dry cleaner instead of relying on throw-away plastic covers for your newly cleaned clothes. If you hang your suits in garment bags, they don't pick up dirt at home, and you won't have to clean them so often.

234 STAY FLUFF-FREE

If you do have to use the dryer, keep it free of fluff by cleaning the filters every week to boost efficiency. Make sure clothes are spun thoroughly in the washing machine before transferring them to the dryer.

235 DRY IT OUT

Dry your washing outside whenever possible. Cutting the number of times you use your dryer by just one load a week could reduce your household carbon dioxide emissions by over 200 pounds a year.

236 DON'T DRY-CLEAN

Most dry-cleaning solvents are potentially poisonous. Chlorine and formaldehyde, for example, are highly toxic and carcinogenic and can remain in your clothes even after you bring them home. Always remove polythene covers and air your clothes thoroughly before returning them to your closet. Where possible, try to buy clothes that you can wash rather than have dry-cleaned.

237 GET ECO-CLEAN

If you have clothes that have to be dry-cleaned, try to locate one of the increasing number of green dry-cleaners, who use nontoxic silicone-based products, which is a much better choice for your health and the environment, too.

238 GET WET

Instead of dry-cleaning your wool and silk clothes, wet-clean them at home by swirling them in cool water using detergent with a pH below 7, then lay flat to dry (for wool) or hang to dry (for silk).

239 WET-CLEAN ONLY

Many clothes that are labeled "dry-clean only" are actually washable by hand with a gentle detergent and cold water, or they can just be gently pressed or ironed. If not, most neighborhoods have wet-clean services that don't use harmful chemicals but rely instead on a combination of steam, pure soap, and vacuuming.

240 ORDER YOUR DISHES

Get the order of play right if you're washing dishes by hand to avoid having to change the water too often. Start with glasses, cutlery, and crockery, then follow with slightly soiled pans and finally very dirty pans. This way you should be able to do the whole amount with one sinkful of water.

241 DON'T LET THE FAUCET RUN

Don't leave the faucet running while you wash up and rinse. Instead, save precious water by putting in the plug and filling up the sink so you wash as many items as possible using the same water. The same goes for rinsing.

242 REUSE YOUR GRAY WATER

Instead of wasting your washing-up water by letting it drain away down the sink, use it for gray water jobs in your home such as watering the garden or try pouring it down the toilet instead of flushing.

243 DON'T RINSE DISHES

There's really no need to rinse your dishes before packing them in the dishwasher. Most modern dishwashers require no pre-rinsing—after all, they are machines designed to wash dirty dishes! Instead, take a stand against rinsing and get into the habit of scraping your plates into a compost or rubbish bin instead.

244 RUNNING ON EMPTY

Every few months, try running a cycle of your dishwasher or washing machine with nothing in it. This process will flush the system through and, as long as you don't do it too frequently, the savings on energy and efficiency will cancel out the extra water usage.

245 BLUE RINSE

If you really have to rinse your dishes before you place them in the dishwasher, choose cold instead of hot water. In the process you'll save vital energy without having to compromise on results.

246 MAKE EVERY LOAD COUNT

Aim to run dishwashers on full loads only. Running half loads is environmentally damaging, uneconomical and won't save you any more time. Machines work best when they are full anyway.

247 DRYING SHAME

Instead of wasting energy by using your dishwasher's drying cycle, simply open the door after the rinse cycle and let the dishes air-dry instead.

248 STAY CLEAN

Cleaning your dishwasher and washing machine filters regularly will help keep them functioning at optimum levels, so they'll use energy in the most efficient way possible and you'll get the best results, too.

bathrooms

249 PANEL IN WARMTH

Choose wood paneling for your bathroom to help keep in heat and reduce air pollution. But make sure you wax rather than varnish it—varnish releases fumes when it gets warm. Wooden floors are a good choice, too.

250 GET A GREEN FLOOR

Linoleum, cork, or terracotta tiles are the best options for a bathroom floor because they're more environmentally friendly than artificial alternatives. Bamboo, too, is beautiful and durable. Augment with an organic cotton bathmat for the ultimate green floor.

251 GO MICROPOROUS

Some bathroom paints, particularly those with antifungal properties, can release fumes when they get warm or moist. Choose water-based microporous paint—it's a lot healthier and kinder to the environment.

252 BATHE IN STYLE

Don't choose a plastic bathtub. Instead, select porcelain or enamel. When it comes to updating your bathroom at some point in the future, you can get the bath re-enameled rather than having to replace it.

253 SHUT THAT DOOR

Close the door when you're having a bath to trap heat in the room and stop the water from cooling down too fast. Otherwise you could be tempted to add more hot water.

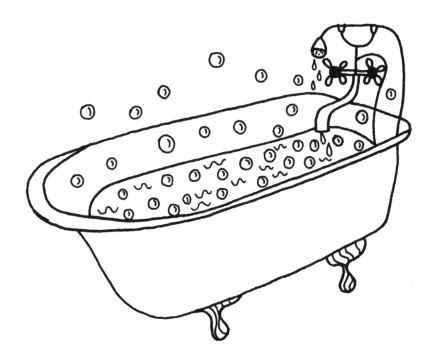

254 DRAFT-PROOF YOUR DOOR

Draft-proof your bathroom door, either by using a removable fabric draft stopper or a brush version that attaches to the bottom of the door. In the absence of drafts the room will stay warm and you won't need to turn up the heating.

255 MINI AT BATHTIME

Instead of choosing a massive bathtub that uses a lot of water, opt for the smallest one possible. If you want to go green, shorter, deeper tubs are better choices because there is less surface area to volume and therefore less heat loss.

256 FIBERGLASS FOLLY

Some bathroom companies still use fiberglass. Avoid it wherever possible as a great lot of energy is wasted during fiberglass manufacture.

257 SLOW-FLOW YOUR SHOWER

Installing a low-flow showerhead helps save water. It may take getting used to, but after a few showers, you won't even notice the difference in water flow.

258 DRY YOURSELF ORGANICALLY

Buy organic, unbleached cotton towels to use after your bath, and try to use the smallest towels possible for the job because they will require less laundering.

259 POWER IT DOWN

To prevent water being wasted, swap your power shower for a normal version or install a water-saving shower head to reduce your water consumption.

260 GO ELECTRIC

As far as energy consumption is concerned, an electric shower (which heats water only as required) is usually a more sound choice than other water heating systems that heat up more water than you need, thereby wasting precious heat energy.

261 SHARE WATER

If you prefer to bathe rather than take a shower, think about sharing water in the family—take it in turns to bathe first, and minimize the soap and shampoo you use. A bathful should be plenty for two children or an adult couple to share.

262 BATHTIME FUN

Bathe your children together in the same water rather than separately. They'll enjoy it more and in the process you'll use half the water. You can even save time by cleaning the bathroom while the kids are in the bath (but don't turn your back on them). You'll be able to get your chores done and keep an eye on them at the same time.

263 SWAP YOUR SHOWER

Did you know that the average shower uses 20 gallons of water, compared to the 40 gallons that's needed for a bath? Simply swapping your baths for showers could save 2,000 gallons of water a year if you take a five-minute shower every day, or double this amount if you shower only every other day.

264 TURN IT OFF

Many people keep the shower running even when they're not actually underneath the water—often for as long as half their showering time. Instead of directing the water against the wall or stepping back, turn it off altogether while you wash or shampoo and then turn the water back on to rinse.

265 GET A VALVE

Go for an ultra-efficient toilet fitted with a low-flush valve rather than a siphon flushing system. It saves water by allowing the cistern to refill during the flush. Most modern toilets are now available with valve-flush systems to give them higher green ratings.

266 DUAL FLUSHING

When it comes to buying a toilet, look for a dual-flush model that allows you to choose between a small and large flush. They use 1.3 gallons of water on a big flush, and under 1 gallon on a small flush. The good news is that you don't need to buy a new toilet—it is possible to attach a dual-flush system to your existing toilet.

267 IN IT TOGETHER

If you live with other people, whenever possible it makes good green sense to try and coordinate your trips to the toilet so you only have to flush once. Even if there's just the two of you, this will cut your flushing water wastage in half.

268 COMPOST YOUR TOILET

If you really want to make your bathroom the greenest room in the house, why not take the major step of installing a compost toilet system? This is a unique system where dry matter and sawdust combine in a pit underneath the toilet to compost all your waste naturally but without smells.

269 FLUSH IT DOWN

Did you know that the average household uses 20–28 gallons of water per day just to flush the toilet? For a water-efficient solution, simply install a low-flush toilet and you'll cut flushing volumes by half. Your state or municipality may even offer tax incentives, rebates, or a voucher if you decide to install a low-flush or ultra low-flush toilet.

270 CHECK FOR LEAKS

You can check your toilet system for leaks by adding a little vegetable dye to the water in your cistern. If any of the dye appears in the toilet bowl without you flushing, then you know you have a leak that is wasting precious water.

271 NO SPONGING

Say no to a real sponge in your bath or shower—it might be soft and natural-looking but if you buy one you are contributing to the stripping of natural products from the ocean floor. Most artificial sponges are made from polyurethane so use a cotton washcloth instead.

65

272 BYE-BYE BIDET

Say no to a bidet—it wastes valuable water and doesn't do a job that you can't do elsewhere in your bathroom. Wipe with moistened toilet paper instead, or use the shower.

273 LIMIT YOUR FLUSHES

Think about whether it's really necessary to flush the toilet every time you visit. Make a rule of thumb only to flush every other time you use the toilet.

274 DON'T FLUSH AT NIGHT

Why not make it a household rule to not flush the toilet at night? That way you'll save water and you won't make noise that might disturb the sleep of others in the house.

275 GET AN ECO CLEANER

Invest in an ecological toilet bowl cleaner that removes mineral deposits and rust without chemicals. Or use a "pod" version that contains minerals and which is dropped into the cistern to prevent unsightly stains and deposits build-up.

276 GET A WATER SYSTEM

Why not consider installing a water-saving system to help you divert water around your home. A common option is to use bathwater or sink run-off, rather than clean water, to flush the toilet.

277 BRUSH UP YOUR WOOD

Don't use a plastic toilet brush. Instead, use wooden brushes with natural bristles that can be washed after use. It's important to wash toilet brushes anyway, rather than leaving them in a stand.

278 SPOT THE SYMBOL

One of the many uses of recycled plastic is to make a variety of items for the home, such as brush or razor handles, or toothbrushes. Look out for the recycled symbol whenever you're replacing your toothbrush.

279 BUMP YOUR BATH

Instead of plastic bath mats, opt for a wooden slatted version. Better still, choose a bath that has added grooves or bumps to stop you slipping so you don't need any other products.

280 BRUSH WITH SOLAR POWER

If you use an electric toothbrush, look for a solar-powered recharger instead of one that plugs into the electrical outlet. And if you must use electric, make sure you unplug it between charging.

281 BUY RECYCLED

Buy recycled toilet paper. You're always going to use it only once before throwing it away, so it doesn't have to be the very best quality.

282 PIN PRICK YOUR SHOWER

Don't allow mineral deposits to build up on your shower head. To keep your shower working efficiently, regularly remove and soak your showerhead in white vinegar to clean. You can poke through any blocked holes with a needle.

283 DECHLORINATE YOUR SHOWER

Chlorine is added to the water to stop microbes from growing. If you're worried about the pollution this could cause in your home, think about investing in a dechlorinating shower instead to prevent you from inhaling unpleasant chlorine fumes while you shower. Use a water filter for all your tap water.

284 GET JUICY

Don't buy cleaning supplies filled with chemicals to treat your bathroom faucets—instead, clear mineral deposits by using a clean, soft cloth soaked in lemon juice. Any stains will disappear in no time at all and the room will smell great, too.

285 SAY NO TO CHLORINE

Most commercial tile cleaners do more harm than good to the environment because they contain chlorine. This is a dangerous chemical with polluting tendencies and an irritant to the eyes, nose and skin. Use baking soda, plus a firm-bristled brush, and plenty of elbow grease instead.

286 SHOWER BEHIND GLASS

When buying a new shower curtain, choose cloth instead of PVC, or better still, go for a glass door or screen as it won't need replacing for many years.

287 VINEGAR AWAY MILDEW

To get rid of mold and mildew without polluting your environment with bleach and antibacterial agents, rub tiles and caulking with a cloth moistened with vinegar and scrub with an old toothbrush.

288 SWITCH IT OFF

Save energy by installing a separate switch for your bathroom fan so it's not linked to the main light and therefore won't come on every time you turn on the light. Then you can make sure you only use it when you really need to.

289 CURTAIN CALL

Don't rely on manufactured cleaning products containing bleach or other harmful chemicals for your shower. Soak shower curtains in salted water before hanging them up and scrub with a paste made with water and baking soda to remove mildew.

290 MINI SERIES

Don't use miniature bottles of soap or shampoo in your own or hotel bathrooms—the packaging is highly energy demanding. Always go for bigger packages.

291 GET BREEZY

To get the excess moisture out of your bathroom, think about installing a wind-operated fan rather than an electric one. It will have the same effect, but won't waste any energy.

292 TRIAL SEPARATION

Get a separate fluorescent light installed by your bathroom mirror, one that isn't linked to the main fan or light in the room. That way, you can see yourself clearly for close-up jobs without having to switch on the main light.

293 DON'T WASH EVERY DAY

Because most shampoos contain detergents that stick around as chemical compounds in waterways, it's most environmentally friendly not to wash your hair every day. It's better for your hair as well. Three times a week should be plenty.

294 DON'T FLUSH HAIR

If strands of hair fall out while you're shampooing, don't flush them down the drain as this will cause the pipes to clog up, increasing your reliance on chemical drain cleaners in the future. Instead, collect it and put in the trash for disposal or use a trap in the drain to catch hair.

295 GET ABSORBENT

Use a high-absorbency towel on your hair before you begin to blow-dry. By removing as much excess water as possible, your blow-drying time will be shorter, which will save on energy. It's also a lot healthier for your hair not to be exposed to direct heat for too long. Choose ultra-soft, high-absorbency towels described as low-twist, no-twist, or microfiber.

296 MAGIC MIXER

Replace any old-fashioned separate hot and cold faucets with a mixer version, which allows you to use the minimum amount of hot water to get your water to the required temperature and so cut down on heat wastage.

297 SUPER-SENSITIVE FAUCETS

The best choice for helping you save water in your sink is a low-flow, sensor-activated faucet that turns on only when it's triggered by your hands. While these were once the domain of public toilets only, many companies now make domestic versions. With a built-in filter, they're also more hygienic and save energy, too.

298 WATER BREAK

Remembering to turn off the faucet while you're brushing your teeth, applying makeup or cleanser, or shaving helps save an incredible amount of water. Turning off the water while you are brushing your teeth can save 2 gallons of water. Try to get into the habit of turning the faucet off whenever the water is not actually needed.

299 MAKE SENSE WITH WATERSENSE

Look for products carrying the Environmental Protection Agency's WaterSense label. In general these will be 20% more water-efficient than theie standart counterparts. Visit www.epa.gov/watersense for more information.

bedrooms

300 FIND A FUTON

Instead of investing in a cheap, mass-produced bed for your spare room, buy a Japanese futon with a cotton mattress and untreated base. It is a much better environmental choice and won't set you back financially either. It can double up as useful daytime seating, too.

301 TIE UP YOUR COMFORTER

When you're choosing a cover for your comforter or duvet, look for cloth tie fastenings or wooden buttons rather than plastic buttons, zippers, or metal fasteners.

302 BED DOWN ORGANICALLY

Choose organic fabrics for your bedding—not only is it a good natural choice to help your mattress breathe (and therefore make it last longer), but you can be sure no chemicals have been used in the manufacturing process. If you're allergic or sensitive to certain chemicals, going organic may be the answer to getting a good night's sleep.

303 SOURCE SUSTAINABLY

Metal beds are thought by some to pick up electromagnetic radiation, so choosing wood is a good option for your health as well as the environment. The greenest choice of all is a wooden bed frame with a slatted base that allows the mattress to breathe. But make sure your wood is sourced sustainably to avoid contributing to deforestation.

304 NATURALLY NICE

Choose a mattress with a wool or cotton topping. Not only are the natural fibers more environmentally friendly but they also enable your body to wick away moisture, helping you to get a more healthy, good night's sleep.

305 BLANKET COVERAGE

The greenest way of all to cover yourself at night is with an organic cotton sheet and secondhand pure wool blankets rather than duvets or new blankets. You can also get blankets made from a hemp-flax blend, both sustainable fibers. Make sure no acid was used in the manufacturing.

306 PUT OUT YOUR FIRES

Don't invest in expensive fire-retardant bed covers. These are manufactured using high amounts of chemicals that will pollute the environment unless they are disposed of carefully. Instead, opt for a thick layer of pure new wool, which is a natural fire extinguisher.

307 ARTIFICIAL INTELLIGENCE

Don't choose synthetic fabrics for your bed linen. You spend a third of your life in bed, so why not treat yourself to natural cotton, linen, or hemp instead? You'll help your skin to breathe more easily as well as getting an extra green point in the process.

308 GET DOWN ON IT

For a relaxing night's sleep, buy a comforter and pillows that are filled with natural down rather than polyester. Down is a natural and sustainable choice, but make sure your down source isn't wasting the birds' bodies—they should be working in partnership with food producers to make full use of the birds.

309 RING YOUR OWN BELL

Choose a traditional clockwork alarm for your bedroom instead of adding to your collection of electrical equipment with an electric or battery-powered alarm clock. It won't let you down if there's a power cut either!

310 STUFF UP YOUR GAPS

If your windows are drafty in the winter and you can't afford to replace them with more efficient versions, recycle old cloths or clothes to plug up the gaps. Cut, roll tightly, and stuff into window gaps to help conserve heat. You can also sew attractive draft stoppers using a long tube of pretty cotton fabric filled with batting to coordinate with your room décor.

311 KEEP YOUR COOL

Make sure you don't overheat your bedroom—not only is it a waste of energy, it's also considered unhealthy to sleep in a room that is too warm. Aim to keep it at 60°F for adults and 65°F for children and the elderly.

312 ADD AN UNDERLAYER

In winter, instead of turning your heating up when the nights start getting colder, add a pure new wool underblanket under your sheet. This will insulate against heat loss and help warm you from beneath.

furniture

313 CHOOSE UNTREATED WOOD

Pressure-treated lumber—a material frequently used for playground equipment—often contains arsenic, a toxin that can rub off onto skin. It can also leach into the soil, where it could poison wildlife. Use untreated wood instead.

314 SOFA SO GOOD

Be sure to check the label before buying a sofa. Soft furnishings containing polyurethane foam are an environmental no-no because of the amount of toxins released during their manufacture. Plus, they can be a fire hazard, too.

315 BE A FIREFIGHTER

Flame-retardant chemicals, thought to be from the manufacture of fire-resistant furniture, have been showing up in animals and humans around the globe. The highest levels have been found in freshwater fish in Virginia. Take other precautions against fire, such as installing extinguishers and alarms and checking your wiring on a regular basis.

316 SIT ON HEMP

Hemp is a great choice for furniture fillings—not only is it easy to produce, long lasting and biodegradable, but it also helps to absorb and combat static build-up caused by electrical equipment in your home. Hemp fiber is extremely durable, long, and strong, and can be woven into natural composites, which can then be formed into anything from containers to furniture.

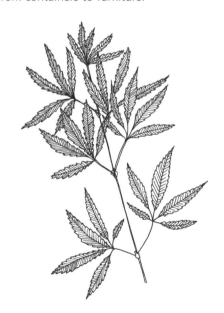

317 OPPOSE DEFORESTATION

The planet has lost nearly half of its forested area in the past 8,000 years, with the majority of this loss occurring in the twentieth century. Between 1980 and 1995 alone, 770,000 square miles of forest were destroyed. Take a stand against those who deplete rainforests by buying your wood from sustainable sources and avoiding tropical hardwoods.

318 FILL IT UP NATURALLY

When you're choosing home furnishings, go for natural fillings such as wool and cotton rather than plastic-based fillings. Not only are they energetically expensive to manufacture, but they do not decompose easily.

319 VISIT AN UPHOLSTERER

Instead of buying a new sofa or armchair every time you change your décor, consider keeping your old furniture and getting it reupholstered. Not only is this a better ecological choice, it's usually cheaper, too.

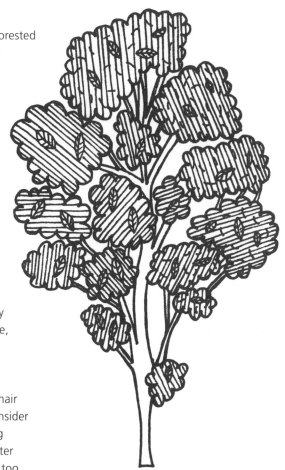

320 HEALTHY FURNITURE

Formaldehyde is a harsh air pollutant and the fumes can be harmful if inhaled, but it's still used in the manufacture of furniture. It can be found in the glues, resins and board materials but also in the foam products used in upholstery. Make sure yours hasn't had formaldehyde added, for the sake of your own health as well as that of the environment.

321 LOBBY FOR LOW INTENSITY

Avoid using formica and melamine in your home as they are very high-intensity plastics—in other words, they take a lot of energy to produce and don't biodegrade, adding to landfill.

322 SAY NO TO MDF

If you're thinking about planning for a greener living space, MDF (medium-density fiberboard) isn't a good choice for a building material in terms of the environment because of the high energy use during its manufacture. If you have no other choice, at least make sure you choose a formaldehyde-free version.

323 NATURALLY WOODY

Wood is the greenest choice for kitchen worktops and for tabletops and other lean-on areas but don't choose ready-treated or varnished versions, which may contain toxins. Instead, choose natural oil or resin finishes.

324 RECLAIM YOUR STYLE

Whenever possible, use reclaimed tiles for your home improvements. But be careful not to buy them if they have toxic coatings, which can release poisons into the environment. This applies particularly around food areas and in the bathroom where water can encourage the leakage of toxins.

325 JOINT ATTEMPT

If you're investing in wooden furniture, such as an armoire or dresser, look for pieces with wooden joints like dovetails rather than metal or other materials. That way, if you ever decided to get rid of it, the whole item will be recyclable or biodegradable. These items can also be found at auctions and second-hand stores, making them ideal recycling and reusing choices.

kitchens

326 GET IT SORTED

If you have problems sorting through your garbage and deciding what to recycle, why not invest in a special dual-receptacle? These have separate compartments for different materials and will help you sort your waste at the point of disposal.

327 BE IN-VENTIVE

Consider adding a closable roof ventilator above or near your refrigerator in the kitchen. This will help vent excess heat from the kitchen area during the summer and then in winter it will help to preserve it. What's more, it's easy to install and use.

328 STRING THEM ALONG

For wet floor cleaning, invest in a loop-end, cotton string mop, rather than a foam or microfiber mop head that will need to be replaced every now and again. The string mop can be thoroughly washed and used for much longer. The looped ends also will make it unlikely that the mop will fray or unravel.

329 BACTERIA BAN

Don't allow yourself to be sucked in by chemical-ridden antibacterial products that claim to reduce the bacteria in your home. Most bacteria are, in fact, killed by hot, soapy water, which is the most environmentally friendly way to keep your house clean. Plain soap, water, baking soda, vinegar, lemon juice, and borax can satisfy most household cleaning needs.

330 CUT DOWN YOUR PLASTIC

Swap plastic containers for stainless steel ones that you can reuse many times. Instead of using microwavable plastic containers, use ceramic microwave-safe versions or glass. Also pack food in brown paper bags or empty bread bags instead of specially made ziploc sandwich bags to cut down on the use of plastic in your kitchen.

331 TIME FOR A KNEE LIFT

Choose knee- or foot-operated faucets for water in your kitchen. These allow you to use only the amount of water you need whenever you wash your hands. They are more hygienic and allow greater control.

332 DON'T WRAP IT UP

Avoid using plastic wrap wherever possible in your kitchen as the manufacturing process is environmentally unfriendly—it takes a lot of energy to produce a single roll. It's much greener to cover food with washable cloths or lids instead.

333 CHEMICAL COVER-UP

Did you know that cellophane is much more environmentally friendly than plastic wrap, foil, and other plastics as it doesn't leach chemicals into food? Likewise, when cellophane goes into landfill or garbage dump after it has been thrown away, it won't leach chemicals into the environment either.

334 GO POTTY

Don't use aluminum pots or pans. Stainless steel or ceramic versions are longer-lasting and healthier alternatives (acidic foods such as tomatoes can absorb aluminum, especially if the pan is badly worn, and aluminum has been associated with Alzheimer's). The manufacture of stainless steel and ceramic is also less harmful to the environment.

335 PAPER THE KITCHEN

Choose parchment paper instead of foil for use in the kitchen wherever you can. It's perfect for covering poultry for roasting, for catching fat in pans, as well as wrapping around fish, vegetables, and cheese for cooking.

336 SAY NO TO FOIL

Because aluminum foil is so thin, it has to go through a whole range of processes during its manufacture. This means it has high environmental cost. Only use foil where it's absolutely necessary, and try to wash and reuse it wherever possible as it is quite strong.

337 GET HEAVY WITH YOUR PANS

Instead of teflon- or plastic-coated pots and pans, invest in a set made of stainless steel or cast iron. They might be a little bit more expensive, but they'll certainly last longer. Cast iron is known for its durability and even heating. Unlike metals that can flake off other types of pans into your food, iron is considered a healthy food additive rather than a harmful one.

338 TURN DOWN YOUR FRIDGE

Your refrigerator uses more energy than pretty much any other appliance. Keep it at its optimum functioning temperature: 38–41°F for the fridge and 0–5°F for the freezer. Any lower and you're wasting energy.

339 GET BEHIND DIRT

Look behind your fridge once in a while—vacuuming or wiping the condenser coils on the back will help reduce dust build-up and make your fridge function more efficiently.

340 IRON FOILINGS

Instead of throwing away your used metal foil, tape it under your ironing board cover using heat-resistant tape instead. The tape will reflect the heat back toward the clothes, meaning you can turn your iron down without losing any of its crease-busting power.

341 REDUCE YOUR METAL

In general, make it a household rule of thumb to reduce the amount of metal cooking implements you use in your kitchen, but remember not to replace them with plastic, which is an even less green option. Wood should always be your number one choice for cooking and serving utensils.

342 MAKE SURE IT'S STEADY

Keep a thermometer in your refrigerator and track it for a week to make sure the temperature isn't fluctuating. If it does not maintain temperatures, your fridge may need to be serviced, or else the food contents could prove a health hazard to your family.

343 STICK TO STICK

Wherever possible, try to avoid nonstick coatings on kitchen implements. They can release toxic fumes if overheated—traces of chemicals used in nonstick pans have even been found in polar bears in the Arctic.

344 CLEAN YOUR FRIDGE

Make sure you wipe out the inside of your fridge every week or so, and stop debris accumulating in corners. A clean fridge can be up to 20% more efficient than a dirty one, meaning you use up less energy to keep it cool. Mix a little baking soda in a small bowl with water and leave it in the fridge to keep everything sweet-smelling, too.

345 RIGHT-SIZE YOUR APPLIANCES

Huge appliances—from six-slice toasters and toaster ovens to chest freezers and double-oven cooking ranges—use more energy and they take up more space. You'll build, heat, and cool additional square footage to accommodate them. If you really don't need the extra capacity, don't buy it.

346 DO AWAY WITH DIRT

Keep your fridge door gasket clean to make sure the seal isn't broken by specks and spots of dried food or congealed substances. Make sure you wipe around gaskets and seals regularly to help the door seal remain airtight.

347 FREEZE THE FRIDGE

Did you know that your refrigerator accounts for more than a third of the domestic appliance energy that's used in your home? If possible, choose a smaller fridge instead and create a pantry in your house to store food that doesn't really need refrigerating.

348 DISPOSE OF FRIDGES CAREFULLY

Make sure you dispose of your old CFC-coolant fridge carefully and responsibly. There are now strict rules on fridge disposal to ensure they are trashed with the least environmental pollution possible in order to minimize CFC leakage into the atmosphere. Most fridges before 1994 use CFCs, but a label on the back of the appliance may list the refrigerant used.

349 SAY NO TO CFC

CFCs (chlorofluorocarbons), which are used in aerosols, refrigerants, and other industrial products, continue to destroy the ozone layer for 100 years after their disposal. The most environmentally friendly fridge to choose is therefore one that uses a hydrocarbon coolant rather than CFC or HCFC.

350 KEEP DOORS CLOSED

It takes three minutes for a fridge to regain its temperature, even after short opening, but much longer if the door has been left open for longer, so remember to close the door while you're preparing food or pouring orange juice.

351 DO IT ALL AT ONCE

When you're cooking, try to take everything you need out of the refrigerator at once rather than making lots of visits. When the door is opened and closed every now and then, cold air escapes every time, so wasting energy. Keep a sign on the refrigerator to remind children and other family members to open the fridge only when necessary and not to leave it open.

352 BOIL ONLY WHAT YOU NEED

Most of us tend to boil twice the amount of water we need every time we turn on an electric kettle. This equates to wasting the energy of around 50 light bulbs. The solution is to fill the kettle up with only the amount of water you actually need, or alternatively use a small-size kettle for boiling water for one.

← HALF   FULL

353 DON'T BE FROSTY

Make sure you defrost your fridge and freezer regularly to help keep them running most efficiently. If ice and debris build up, it takes more energy to keep it at the right temperature. Even auto-defrost fridges and freezers should be defrosted at the first sign of ice build-up.

354 KEEP IT COOL

Never put hot food or drinks into the fridge to cool as it will raise the internal temperature and will use a lot of energy to bring it to the right temperature. Let it cool to room temperature naturally before storing it in the refrigerator.

355 STAY OUT OF THE SUN

Make the most of the natural shade and cool spots in your home. Don't place your refrigerator in a sunny spot and keep it away from the cooking range to make sure you don't heat it up artificially and make it work harder.

356 INSULATE WITH FOIL

To keep the desired temperature around your fridge and freezer, insulate surfaces with used and washed aluminum foil to make sure precious energy isn't wasted.

357 DON'T OVERFILL

Fridges work most efficiently when they are just full enough for items to hold the cold temperature but not so full that air circulation is limited. About three-quarters full is usually best. Keeping this rule in mind will also help prevent buying too much food, which may spoil and be wasted.

358 STACK AND CLOSE

After you've stacked your fridge following a supermarket shop, try to leave the door closed for as long as possible so the newly stacked, less cold food can be brought down to the right temperature quicker.

359 QUALITY OVER QUANTITY

When it comes to gadgets for the home, buy to last rather than to dispose. It's worth spending a little bit more if an item will last twice as long.

360 SUCK OUT THE AIR

Invest in a freezer with a vacuum system that sucks air out as you close the door, reducing build-up of ice and helping the freezer to stay efficient. Those with high-energy ratings should have this as standard feature.

361 PARK YOUR FREEZER

If you've got a garage, put your freezer there. A garage is usually the coolest place in a home—it will require far less energy to keep your food frozen when the room temperature is already low.

362 CHILL OUT

Your fridge is probably the single appliance that uses most energy. To check that it seals properly, shut the door on a dollar bill—if the paper slips when the door is closed, it's time to replace your seals.

363 COOK ON GAS

Gas is a more efficient fuel than electricity, so choose a gas oven range—you will use less energy to cook the same dish. According to a recent study, 96% of professional chefs prefer using a gas cooktop.

364 BE ENERGETIC

Make sure you check and compare energy
ratings before buying large appliances
like refrigerators and freezers. These tell
you how many kilowatt hours of energy it
uses per month, and are invaluable when
planning your greener kitchen.

365 BURN, BABY, BURN!

Use your cooktop sensibly to try and
minimize the number of burners
or rings you use at a time. For
example, if you're cooking rice or
potatoes, you can steam vegetables
above them rather than using a
separate burner. One-pot dishes also
only use one burner for a meal.

366 SWITCH TO SIMMER

Remember to turn down the
heat after your dish has started
boiling, especially when cooking
vegetables. Lightly boiling,
simmering water is the same
temperature as a roaring boil,
but requires only a small flame
to keep it going.

367 PUT THE KETTLE ON

Instead of boiling water in pans or in a cooktop kettle, use an electric kettle—it consumes half the amount of energy to heat the same amount of water. Don't just use it for hot drinks, but for any water you need boiling for cooking.

368 BROIL A LITTLE

Try to invest in an oven that has a half-broiler function so you can switch on only half the broiler for smaller cooking jobs instead of heating up the whole grill every time. This means you won't need a separate toaster oven for small jobs.

369 SPARK IT UP

If your cooktop or grill doesn't have a spark ignitor, don't waste matches. Instead, use an old lighter, or buy a spark-maker.

370 PUT A LID ON WATER

Water will boil more quickly, and therefore efficiently, if there is a lid on the pan. Use a lid for all your cooking to avoid heat wastage and evaporation, particularly where liquids are concerned.

371 BE AN OVEN DISH

Don't waste energy preheating your oven; most ovens don't need it. For pastries and cakes, preheating for 10 minutes is usually plenty. When cooking roasts and casseroles turn off your oven approximately 15 minutes early—the heat left in the oven will finish the job.

372 GET A GLASS DOOR

Choose an oven with a glass door and, preferably, a light so that you can check on the progress of food without opening the door and losing valuable heat. Your attempts at baking cakes, muffins, and soufflés (that run the risk of falling flat when the oven door is opened too soon) stand a better chance of being successful, too.

373 STRIKE WHILE THE IRON IS HOT

Don't waste a hot oven. As ovens take a lot more energy to heat from cold than to keep hot, try to cook several nights' worth of cooking in one go, so you end up using the oven intensely only once every few days. Reheat meals in the microwave.

374 COOK IN THE SUN

For the greenest choice in oven ranges, choose a solar or hybrid solar oven that uses retained heat and solar energy to cook food. They are much more efficient but cooking takes twice as long. Alternatively, build an old-fashioned haybox; they can be fun to try when you're on an outdoor vacation.

375 CUT YOUR ENERGY OUTPUT

The refrigerator is the biggest power user in most homes. To ensure yours is more energy-efficient, make sure the energy-saver switch is on during the summer and off during the winter. If you are buying one, choose an Energy Star one with a freezer at the top or bottom, not on the side. Doing without extras like auto defrost and ice makers can save up to 60% more energy.

376 A REAL TURN-OFF

Turn everything off when you go to bed. If you're leaving some appliances running to make the most of cheap electricity after you go to bed, invest in a timer switch to cut off the power after they have finished so they don't run through the night.

377 SIZE MATTERS

To avoid wasting energy from your cooktop, match the size of the burner to the size of the bottom of the pan. This way you will use the minimum amount of energy to heat your food.

378 DON'T COOK FROM FROZEN

Microwaving food from frozen takes more electricity than from room temperature, so let nature do the defrosting rather than relying on your oven. Simply leave your food in the fridge or room to defrost before cooking. Do this in the morning before you leave for work in order to resist the temptation to cook from frozen when you get home.

379 MICROWAVE IT

Microwave ovens are the most environmentally friendly way you can cook. The reason is that they cook faster but also at far lower power than other ovens. Unfortunately microwave ovens often don't produce the most appetizing food. For an oven-baked taste, use the microwave first then finish off in the oven or under the broiler.

380 CATCH THE WAVE

A microwave oven uses 14% less energy than a conventional oven, which could save you precious pennies. It's more efficient when you heat up larger amounts rather than lots of little quantities.

381 SLOW ON THE UPTAKE?

A slow cooker is extremely energy efficient— its electricity consumption is roughly that of a light bulb! And because the whole meal can be cooked in one pot, it reduces further energy wastage.

382 TOUCH WOOD

Choose wooden cutting boards, which have natural antibacterial properties, rather than plastic ones with added antibacterial protection. These boards not only pollute the environment during their manufacture but also produce toxins during use.

383 GLASS IT UP

If you have to invest in an electric blender, choose one made of glass and stainless steel rather than plastic. It will last longer and is less damaging to the environment to produce.

384 MOULI ROUGE

To save electricity, use a hand-turned mouli instead of an electric blender for pureeing vegetables and fruit. (It has the added advantage that it won't make your mashed potatoes go gloopy!)

385 SPLASH ON STEEL

Rather than painting the area behind your sink with moisture-repelling paint, which can contain potentially hazardous fungicides, choose a stainless steel surface—it will last for years.

386 GET HANDY IN THE KITCHEN

Use manual alternatives in the kitchen whenever you can for machine tasks like juicing and mixing. For tasks like grinding that can only be done by machine, try and do larger amounts less often.

387 BRUSH NATURALLY

Replace your plastic disposable dishwashing brush with a wooden one with natural bristles. Even better, buy one with a replaceable head so you throw away as little as possible when it wears out.

388 RADON RADAR

Some granites contain radon gas, which can sometimes emit radioactive particles into the atmosphere. If you have granite in your kitchen, make sure you get it checked.

389 SINK INTO THE SINK

Try to cut down on nonessential plastic use in your home. Don't buy a plastic bowl for your sink, for example. It really isn't necessary—wash up straight in the sink.

390 GO E-CLOTH CRAZY

Instead of a traditional kitchen cloth, choose a reusable e-cloth, which is made from millions of tiny fibers with such a good natural cleaning effect that only water is needed to clean grease, smears, or grime from absolutely anywhere.

391 STEEL YOUR KITCHEN

Stainless steel is a great choice if you're designing a new kitchen and don't like wood. It does have high energy requirements to produce but it's very hardwearing and can be recycled many times to produce different items.

living rooms

392 DON'T STAND BY

Turn appliances off instead of leaving them on standby, which can actually use almost as much energy as leaving them on full.

393 GET OUT OF THE SUN

If you live in a hot climate, avoid overuse of your air conditioning by planting trees or putting up structures that help shade sun-facing doors and windows.

394 GO SOLO WITH LIGHTS

Instead of filling multi-light fixtures with lower wattage bulbs, swap them for just one higher wattage bulb. Or better still, swap your light fixture for one that uses a single bulb, which uses less electricity.

395 SHUT UP DRAFTS

In the winter, use wooden shutters or heavy drapes to block out drafts coming in from windows at night when temperatures drop and the wind often picks up. This way you don't have to keep your heating running so high (or at all) at night.

396 GET A CLEAR VIEW

Instead of dark lampshades and a high-powered bulb to shine through, opt for clear or very light shades that can take a lower wattage bulb and still produce the same amount of light.

397 USE ONLY WHAT YOU NEED

Use electric light in your home according to need rather than tradition—you probably don't need bright lights in every room. Often a desk light or bedside lamp will do just as well, and uses less wattage. Try to do jobs that require more light during the daylight hours when the sun is strongest, leaving evening hours for relaxing.

398 JUTE FROM THE HIP

One of the most environmentally friendly fabrics you can use on your floor is natural grass matting like sisal or jute, which is easy to produce, cheap to manufacture, hardwearing, and totally biodegradable. They're a good choice for areas that are subjected to a lot of wear and tear, such as halls and stairs.

399 GO FOR THE BURN

Create an environmentally friendly natural light by burning aromatherapy candles made from soy or vegetable wax and essential oils. These contain no toxic chemicals and will help you relax naturally in your home and provide ambient lighting.

400 SNUG AS A BUG IN A RUG

Sheepskin rugs are a great choice for the home, as they hold onto warmth and are fantastic insulating fabrics, shielding against drafts and heat loss. Keep them well laundered to fluff up the hairs and so improve insulation.

401 PLANT THE BALANCE

Make sure you include plants in your home to keep the atmosphere balanced. Try to include one plant for every piece of electromagnetic equipment in your home, particularly large items like your television and sound system.

402 MEGA MOISTURE

Humidity levels are important in rooms, not only because the water droplets in the air help your room to hold onto its heat, but also for general health and static reduction. Use bowls of water with a few drops of lemon or orange juice or some rose petals.

403 OIL YOUR CARPETS

Don't use vacuuming powder on your carpets to keep them fresh. They contain talc and chemicals that pollute the air. Use a water spray with a few drops of your favorite essential oil instead.

404 BOTANIC BOOST

Choose plants that are particularly good at removing harmful compounds from the air to help purify the air you breathe in. Ivy, lily, and rubber plant are all good detoxing choices.

405 WATER RECYCLING

Recycle the water left over after cooking vegetables to water houseplants or patio plants and enrich them with valuable vitamins and minerals.

406 KEEP FILTER WATER

When you're installing a new water filter, don't throw away the two jugfuls of water you have to run through the filter before use. It's ideal for watering your houseplants.

407 BE A WINDOW GAZER

The areas in front of the windows are the lightest places in your home but often they are not fully utilized. Consider having a window seat installed in the rooms you use most often, so you can make the most of natural light.

lawn care

408 BE A SHARP OPERATOR

Keep your mower blades sharpened; blunt blades will tear grass rather than cut it, making cutting the grass more time- and energy-consuming. Damaged grass also needs more water than healthy grass.

409 HARDY GRASS

For a lawn that needs less watering, choose well-adapted, hardy, and disease-resistant varieties of grass such as ryegrass or bluegrass, or zoysia or bermuda grass. This will help you save water without a noticeable difference in the appearance of your lawn. Watering in the morning when there is less chance of evaporation will help you conserve water.

410 MAGIC MIX

Fine-blade fescue requires even less fertilizer and water than bluegrass or ryegrass. It's a good idea to have a mix of two or three different grass species for your lawn.

411 CATCH THE RAIN

Put a barrel under your gutter drain to catch rainwater. Using this to water your garden not only saves on your water bill, but your plants and lawn will get the benefit of the natural minerals contained in rain.

412 DIVERT YOUR GRAY WATER

Don't waste your bath water after you've finished. If you set up a bath water diverter system to pipe away your dirty bath water for use in your landscaping, you won't have to use a hosepipe or sprinkler system to irrigate your lawn.

413 GET GOLDEN BROWN

In a drought, don't waste water trying to revive a lawn that is beginning to turn brown; it will revive on its own when it starts to rain again and water levels in the soil top up.

414 DON'T OVERWATER

Be careful not to overwater your lawn. If you do, you run the risk of shallowing the roots, leading to a vicious circle whereby your grass needs more and more water but gets weaker and weaker at water uptake. Err on the dry side when watering your lawn and ensure your sprinklers or water system treats the whole area uniformly; underground sprinkler systems ensure the entire area is treated and waste is minimal.

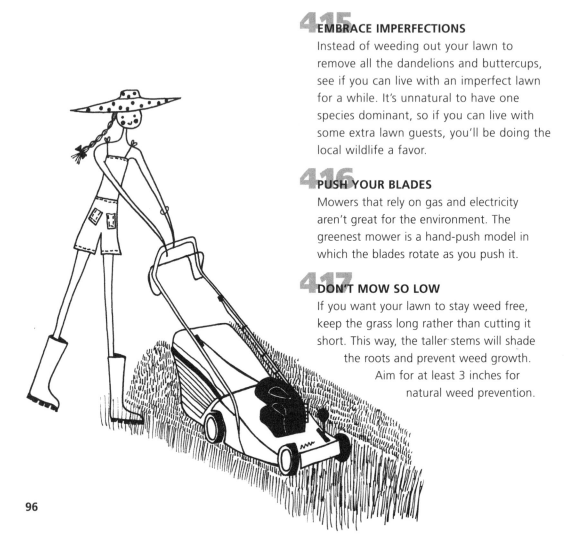

415 EMBRACE IMPERFECTIONS

Instead of weeding out your lawn to remove all the dandelions and buttercups, see if you can live with an imperfect lawn for a while. It's unnatural to have one species dominant, so if you can live with some extra lawn guests, you'll be doing the local wildlife a favor.

416 PUSH YOUR BLADES

Mowers that rely on gas and electricity aren't great for the environment. The greenest mower is a hand-push model in which the blades rotate as you push it.

417 DON'T MOW SO LOW

If you want your lawn to stay weed free, keep the grass long rather than cutting it short. This way, the taller stems will shade the roots and prevent weed growth. Aim for at least 3 inches for natural weed prevention.

418 GROW YOUR GRASS

Allow your grass to grow high, to at least 1.5 inches before you cut it, or the grass will be weakened because the roots won't get a chance to deepen into the soil if the top of the grass is continually being cut.

419 LET CLIPPINGS LIE

Leave your clippings after mowing the lawn rather than collecting them with a mower bag or raking it away, as this will help feed and replenish soil. But don't do this if it's very cold or damp or if the clippings are very long, as they might suffocate the grass.

420 TINKLE YOUR SPRINKLE

Sprinkler systems use as much water in an hour as a family of four do in a whole day—make it a rule of thumb not to use them. Instead, use the hose for short periods or even a watering can.

outdoor decoration & ambience

421 PERFECT MOTION

To save on electricity, fit motion sensors to your outdoor lights so they only go on when they are needed.

422 LEADING LIGHTS

Make sure you choose garden lights that are photovoltaic, meaning they run from solar power rather than using up electricity. There are many different types on the market, from plant level lighting to security spotlights.

423 WHEEL YOUR REFUSE

Garbage cans, wheel trash cans, and recycling containers aren't the prettiest sight, so give some thought to where they're going to be placed on your property. One solution is to build a simple slatted screen or shelter out of reclaimed lumber (also a great material for building fences).

424 DO IT WITH FLARE

Instead of electric lights in your garden, burn garden tiki torches. They last for many hours on just a small amount of oil, while releasing next to no polluting smoke. There are even solar versions. Don't go for wax candles though—they burn too quickly.

425 PUMP UP THE SUN

If you have a water feature in your garden, make sure your water pump runs on solar power rather than batteries or electricity. Even the darkest days will yield enough power to keep it running.

426 FEATURE YOUR WATER

Check water features regularly for leaks and damage. Also make sure they recirculate water rather than it running off.

427 ON THE ROCKS

Choose local rocks for your garden to avoid the large energy costs of transporting stones long-distance. Local plant species will also be better suited to the color and appearance of local rocks and stones.

428 TERRACE YOUR GARDEN

Help avoid water loss due to exposure by gardening on different levels. Tiers and terraces stop water from draining away and help the soil to hold onto more water.

429 BREAK UP THE WIND

Install windbreaks in the form of trellises and boxwood hedges to protect plants in your garden from the drying effect of wind. Helping them hang onto precious moisture means you won't need to water them as often.

430 DON'T LET IT FREEZE

It's unnecessary to heat up your pond in the winter—almost all fish will survive at low temperatures, provided the water doesn't freeze over. Place a rubber ball on the surface to prevent this from happening.

431 LEAVE NO STONE UNTURNED

Although limestone is a natural product, the quarrying process is very harmful to many species of rare plants and butterflies. Many of these species are fast becoming endangered, so avoid using limestone.

432 POT YOUR PLANTS

Make your own plant pots by reusing large
plastic yogurt and ice-cream containers
instead of throwing them away. Simply
put holes in them and hide them inside a
"show" cache pot made of ceramic.

433 HEDGE YOUR BETS

Instead of erecting a high garden fence,
plant shrubs or a hedge that will allow wild
animals to pass from one garden to another.
If you want more privacy, you can put up
a fence above the hedge, but try to 1 foot
free at the bottom.

434 GET A GRASS SEAT

The greenest garden seat of all is one
made of—you guessed it—grass! Create
a turf table and chairs using chicken wire
and rest assured you've got the greenest
furniture in town!

435 FEED THE BIRDS

Apart from being an attractive addition to
the garden, a birdhouse made of reclaimed
wood will attract birds for you to watch and
promote a natural habitat.

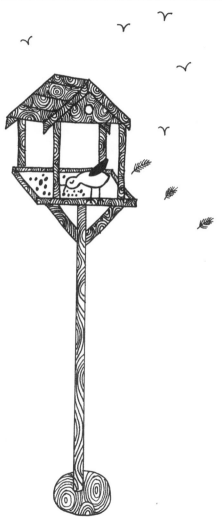

436 RECLAIM YOUR PATIO

If you're having a garden patio laid, look for reclaimed stone or bricks as these have less of an environmental impact—they won't need to travel far to you and you don't have to think about manufacture costs either as you are reusing them.

437 SUPPORT THE FORESTS

If you choose garden furniture made from wood plundered from tropical forests, you are contributing to deforestation. Use a sustainable wood such as oak instead.

438 CAST YOUR NET NEARBY

Cast-iron garden furniture is a good green choice because of its durability—you won't need to replace it soon. But make sure you check how far it has traveled from the manufacturer and buy locally if possible.

439 CHOOSE PAINT CAREFULLY

Be careful about the paint you use on garden furniture, fences, and sheds. Some paints contain chemicals that can leach into the soil, causing damage to the very plants and animals you're trying to encourage.

440 GET SYNTHETIC

The latest green substance on the market is synthetic wood, created from recycled plastics. Use it for fence posts and panels, trellises and areas you intend to cover with climbing plants.

441 BUILD YOUR OWN GRILL

The kindest way to barbecue at home is to make your own built-in grill with old bricks or a recycled drum. This way you're not buying new and you won't have to replace it for many, many years.

442 BUY LOCAL CHARCOAL

Next time you're planning on lighting up a charcoal grill, buy your charcoal from a local, well-managed woodland where you're sure trees are managed responsibly.

443 PRESERVE YOUR FENCE POSTS

Wood preserver contains some harsh and potent chemicals. So instead of treating your posts with it, set them in metal shoes that will protect them from decomposing, or set them in concrete for a permanent solution.

444 DON'T USE CREOSOTE

Don't use creosote wood preservative for your garden wood because it can leach into the soil and give off vapors. This can continue for up to seven years after the application. Instead, choose preservers based on boron, zinc, and copper, which are less harmful.

445 OIL YOUR OUTDOOR WOOD

Linseed oil is an excellent wood preserver for garden furniture. Not only is it totally rainproof but it is also nourishing—so you can be sure your wood will be kept in tip-top condition, whatever the weather outside. Linseed oil is completely natural so you don't have to worry about chemicals either.

446 LEAVE IT ALONE

It is fine to leave your wooden garden furniture in contact with grass or soil without treating it with chemicals. Woods such as oak and chestnut will last up to 20 years before they start to rot, and even untreated pine will last up to five years.

447 SPRINKLE AWAY FLEAS

If you've got a dog kennel in your garden that you want to keep flea-free without using harmful chemicals, simply give the floor a sprinkling of salt to keep the pests at bay and your pooch happy and healthy.

planting & growing

448 RING THE CHANGES

Try not to have one dominant species in your landscaping, as this encourages an over-run of certain types of pest. For the lawn, try using several types of grass and make sure you break it up with different flower beds to encourage diversity.

449 GO NATIVE

Plant local plants in your garden rather than ones from a different climate. Native species are well adjusted to local weather conditions and need less water and maintenance than species introduced from elsewhere. Local wildlife will also be better suited to these.

450 PLANT A TREE

Give up 10 square feet of your land by planting a tree. Trees soak up carbon dioxide and help keep the atmosphere clean. If you don't have the space, use a pot on a balcony or near a window.

451 NO BREAKING WITH TRADITION

Don't go for hybridized newer varieties of garden plants if you can find traditional varieties. Traditional varieties almost always provide better food for insects.

452 DON'T PLUNDER THE WILD

Make sure that when you're buying flowers and vegetables for your garden you don't buy seeds, plants, or bulbs harvested from the wild. The countryside is continually being stripped of its natural plant species for gardens. If you are unsure of the source, buy them at a reputable place and ask.

453 CULTIVATE MOSSES

Don't use sphagnum moss as a lining for your hanging baskets, because it is harvested from moss marshes, which are endangered habitats essential for a wide range of wildlife species. Use cultivated mosses instead.

454 DIG YOURSELF GREEN

Digging is perhaps the single most important thing you can do to condition your soil. Use a shovel or hoe to turn over and break up soil. This will add air pockets, which help to repel root-dwelling insects and oxygenate soil, which in turn helps plants set down healthy roots.

455 MAKE YOUR OWN COMPOST

Instead of buying peaty compost, make your own compost using garden cuttings and kitchen peelings which would otherwise be thrown away. Yard trimmings, leaves, and selected food scraps can all be composted, including fruit scraps, vegetable scraps, coffee grounds, stale bread, and eggshells. Do not include meat, bones, or fat. Compost makes an excellent growing medium for seeds and plants and acts as soil enricher.

456 VARIETY'S THE SPICE OF LIFE

It's more natural—and healthier—to include several species of plant in your garden. Think of planting more natural alternatives to grass, such as ground cover (which will reduce weeds) and vegetables.

457 HEAP O' COMPOST

If you throw away your kitchen waste (vegetable and fruit peelings and cereals) or use a kitchen waste-disposal system, it will only add to landfill and pollute waterways. Composting the waste is the most environmentally friendly option. Refrain from adding cooked food as it attracts vermin. Materials that should only be composted in limited amounts include: wood ashes, which is a source of lime; sawdust, which requires extra nitrogen; plants treated with herbicides (the chemicals need time for thorough decomposition); and shredded nonrecyclable paper.

458 HEAP UP YOUR LEAVES

Don't burn your leaves in the autumn as this contributes to air pollution. Instead, add them to a compost heap where they can biodegrade and enhance your soil in years to come. Fallen leaves carry 50% to 80% of the nutrients a tree extracts from the soil and air, including carbon, potassium, and phosphorus. A mulch of leaves spread over a garden limits weed growth, adds organic matter, and protects the soil.

459 FORK YOUR SOIL

Forking compost and other organic material into your garden soil will help drainage because it breaks up clumps of hard earth to encourage better drainage, and it boosts circulation and humidity levels, resulting in less watering. Adding compost can overcome some typical soil problems as it can help improve clay soils by making them lighter and by helping sandy soils retain water. Composting supplies nutrients to plants and encourages strong healthy growth.

460 PAPER CHASE

If you have a compost heap, don't forget to add dry items like newspaper. The best way to get the right balance is to collect kitchen waste in sheets of newspaper, fold them up, and then add to the heap. Shredded paper will break down much easier. It is common to add too much newspaper, so recycle it instead if you have a lot you need to dispose of. Don't add glossy, laminated, treated, or colored pages, such as magazines or comics, to your compost.

461 WORM YOUR WAY INDOORS

Another composting option is to invest in an indoor wormery. This turns your kitchen scrapings and peelings into small amounts of rich compost to use on houseplants and your garden.

COMPOST

462 JOIN A LOCAL PROGRAM

If you don't want a compost bin or heap in your garden or you haven't got space, consider joining your county's backyard compost program. In many areas you can choose to either deliver waste or have it collected from your doorstep. It's then made into compost used in local recreation areas. Some organizations, such as Starbucks Coffee, will hand out their organic waste if you ask them; it usually comes in large amounts so if you are an urban composter you will need to share it with someone.

463 HELP YOUR HEAP

Protect your compost heap from the rain with a rain cover. If it gets too wet, the compost composition is ruined. Or buy a composting bin with a lid to keep your compost protected from the elements.

464 BURY THE GOODS

If you are worried about flies being attracted to your compost heap, make a hole in the center and bury your kitchen waste in the middle of it to hinder flies and other pests.

465 PEEL AWAY PESTS

To keep your compost heap fresh and keep insects at bay, try adding lemon peel and basil, both of which are smells that flies and other insects find repelling. It will make the heap smell sweeter to your nose as well!

466 BIN THE COMPOST

If you live in an urban area and want to start your own composting system, invest in a sturdy compost bin with a sealable lid to keep rodents out. Rats, seagulls, and other vermin can ruin the composition of compost. Place it on a balcony or outside deck and put an extra lid or tray underneath the container as a drip tray. Don't use compost as a replacement for potting soil as it is too heavy; mix about one part compost with three parts potting or topsoil.

467 FORK OUT FOR QUALITY COMPOST

Turn your compost with a fork every six to eight weeks and leave in a warm place for best results. Or invest in a compost bin with a turning system to keep everything moving around regularly. Temperatures of about 122°F are best.

468 ROOT OUT MORE WATER

Avoid water loss from your soil by making sure you plant long-rooted plant species that draw water from the deeper layers of the soil instead of a lot of short-rooted varieties that will compete for the same water.

469 AVOID THE CROWDS

Don't overcrowd plants in your vegetable garden or flowerbeds—naturally, plants leave one another a bit of space to avoid passing on pests and disease. Help your garden to be healthier by using space wisely and you'll need less chemical intervention.

470 STOP THE SPREAD

The minute you notice one of your plants is diseased, get rid of it to avoid it passing on the disease. Make sure you dispose of it away from other plants—adding it to your compost could encourage the disease to spread.

471 HAVE A GOOD MEAL

If you must use fertilizer on your garden, don't choose peat or synthetic alternatives, but use an organically derived variety like fish and bone meal or seaweed-based products.

472 MULCH YOUR BORDERS

To reduce your water usage in the garden, add mulch to your soil. Not only does this help the soil retain moisture, meaning you won't need to waste water by using your garden hose or sprinkler, but it also protects the soil from scorching and encourages it to hold onto minerals.

473 SOAK YOUR SOIL

Don't soak plants with water from a hose—instead, use a porous soaker hose irrigation system that will leak water to plants slowly, ensuring they can make use of every last drop. You can buy irrigation systems in most garden centers and nurseries.

474 MAKE A MEADOW

If you've got space, consider creating a wildflower meadow or wild area in your backyard by planting wild flowers or seed. Local wild flowers will attract butterflies, bees, and other desirable insects.

475 GET YEAR-ROUND COLOR

Choose plants that flower and bear fruit at different times of the year to make your outdoor space attractive to wildlife all year round. A great idea is to plant a winter and summer climber over a trellis so you'll have color whatever the season.

476 SET UP A TRICKLE

Make your own trickle irrigation system using a hose with pinholes in it set on low flow. This is much healthier for the soil than soaking it once a day or week, as it more closely mimics natural weather systems and will reduce disease.

477 WATER AT NIGHT

Instead of watering plants in the heat of the day when lots of water is lost through evaporation, mimic their natural state by watering in the early morning or evening, when dew would naturally form. The plants will be able to take up more water because the sun won't encourage evaporation and you'll waste less.

478 HERBS BETWEEN FLOWERS

Fresh herbs are easy to grow in your garden and help encourage bees, butterflies, and other useful garden insects. Herbs are a great choice for planting between other flowers or vegetables to increase diversity. Choose basil, oregano, cilantro, sage, and tarragon alongside vegetables that will remind you to use them together.

479 LESS IS MORE

Instead of watering plants a little every day, give them more water less often—1 inch a week is better than a little every day as it mimics natural rainfall conditions and will encourages efficient water use by plants.

480 TAKE THE LEAD

With the rising price of municipal water and summer drought restrictions, many people are harvesting rainwater to save money and protect supplies. Make sure you don't get the rainwater from lead roofs or gutters because it may contain compounds that could be harmful if they get into the ecosystem.

481 DIG UP A DWARF

Don't give up on the idea of growing your own vegetables because you haven't got enough space for a vegetable patch or herb garden—dwarf varieties of most vegetables can be grown in containers and will withstand pretty much any weather condition, except for extreme wind. Even roof-top gardens or container-grown plants can provide extra fresh food during the summer months.

482 CONTAIN YOURSELF

Don't buy new plastic plant containers to do jobs in your garden—use old sinks, car tires, cracked terracotta pots, and other used items instead of buying new. Old salad and mixing bowls can make great herb pots.

483 GREEN FINGERS

If you're buying grow-bags for your tomatoes, make sure you buy peat-free versions as the removal of peat from marshes destroy precious wildlife habitats. Choose organic, as tomatoes are quite watery, which means they hold onto soil toxins.

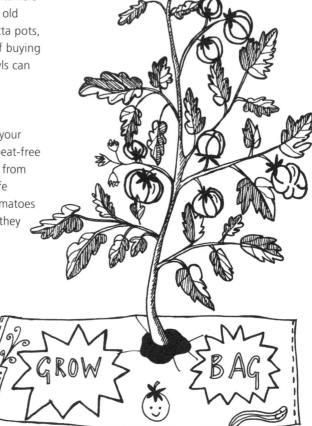

484 KEEP POTATOES HEALTHY

Potatoes hold onto toxins if pesticides are used. Buy organic or, if you want to protect your home-grown potatoes from flea beetles, try interplanting with collard greens. Never add lime before planting potatoes, as this can encourage scab disease.

485 PRIVATE PATCH

If you want to grow your own vegetables but don't have the space, find out if there are any community gardening projects where you could start up your own vegetable patch. There may also be urban gardening programs operating in your neighborhood, where you can spend time growing vegetables and take some of the fruits of your labor away.

486 KEEP FAMILIES APART

To ensure that your vegetable patch grows naturally and you get the best from your crops, avoid planting similar species (like broccoli and cabbage) together because they compete for nutrients. Instead, create an even spread of different plant varieties.

487 SQUASH IN THE VEGETABLES

If you don't want to create a whole separate vegetable patch in your garden, or if you haven't got space, simply plant them in among your flower beds and borders to make the most of your backyard space.

488 GO FOR THE HOT STUFF

Maximize your warm windowsills by growing Mediterranean herbs and peppers. They are suited to the hot, dry conditions and will give you good, long yields.

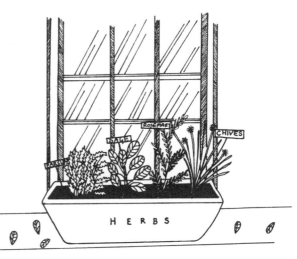

489 APPLE OF YOUR EYE

One of the best things you can do in your backyard is to plant a fruit tree. Apple, plum, and pear trees are all hardy and will produce fruit as well as provide a home for birds and other wildlife.

490 LIVING POTS

Instead of buying new "old look" pots, you can age your current terracotta containers by covering them in yogurt every other evening for a few weeks to encourage lichens.

491 BOX UP YOUR EGGS

Don't throw away empty cardboard egg boxes—they make a great green replacement for plastic seedling trays and because they're biodegradable, you don't have to remove them when you plant the seedlings out.

492 GROW SOME SEEDLINGS

Some types of plastic, like that used for fruit and vegetable packaging, can't be recycled. To help minimize your waste, get creative with ideas for reusing them, like growing herbs or sowing seedlings in the containers.

493 GET TOOLED UP

Choose garden tools made from
sustainable wood or recycled plastic and
rubber, not PVC, especially for water-
containing items like rain buckets and
hoses, as well as compost bins.

494 HOME-GROWN HARVEST

Reduce the effect of
transportation pollution from
your shopping by growing
your own vegetables. Even
a small plot of land or
container-grown plants will
make a beneficial effect.

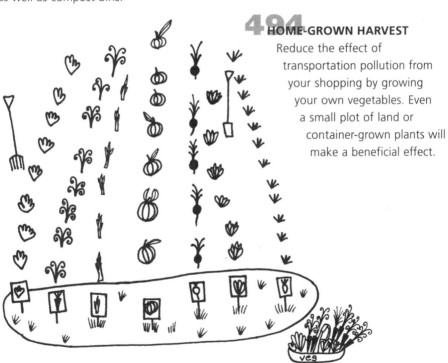

weeds & pests

485 ROOT OFF THE PROBLEM

Don't use weed killer in your garden. It might appear to be the quick-and-easy option but could make your weeds grow back stronger. Weeding by hand is very effective as it weakens the weed at the root. Pull up weeds before they go to seed and self-spread and make sure you get the whole weed, including the root.

496 MAT YOUR WEEDS

Instead of weedkiller, use mulch between flowers to prevent weeds getting a hold in the first place; for really hardy weeds that grow through the mulch, use a weed-mat or cardboard.

497 BE A CHIVE BUNNY

Aphids hate chives, so they're a great choice to plant alongside your roses to help keep the pests away. (If your roses are already suffering from aphids, pick them off by hand instead of using pesticide. Remember to wear gloves to protect your fingers from the thorns.)

498 BUILD A HOTEL

Try to leave an area of dead wood in your garden as an insect "hotel," where natural insect life is encouraged to develop. It doesn't have to be large—a few broken-up logs will do and you'll soon reap the wildlife benefits.

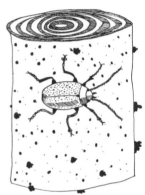

499 DUST TO DUST

Pyrethrum dust, which is made from chrysanthemums, will kill your unwanted aphids but it can also damage some susceptible plants and cause damage to other, beneficial insects. Use it with care.

500 PINCH AWAY PESTS

The best way to remove pests from plants is to pinch them off with your fingers. You'll be sure they'll never come back without having to resort to poisons.

501 DON'T USE PESTICIDES

To give the local wildlife a helping
hand, make it a rule of thumb not to
use pesticides or fertilizers in your garden.
Even small amounts can build up in the
food chain and cause harm to birds
and mammals.

502 KEEP SPIDERS HAPPY

Don't kill spiders—they are important
pest killers. Try and co-exist with them in
both your backyard and in your home.
They're doing you a favor by keeping your
space pest-free.

503 PELT WITH SALT

Although slugs are undesirable, birds and
other wildlife might eat up to ten slugs a day,
so the toxins in slug pellets may build up and
be harmful to them. Remove slugs by hand,
or use salt pellets, which are wildlife-friendly.

504 DEVILISH DETERRENT

According to garden mythology, the
best way to remove the pests from your
garden is to collect slugs and create a liquid of
their dead remains, allowing it to decompose
in natural rainwater for a few weeks. Then
use the liquid around plants to protect them.

505 SQUIRT WITH SOAP

Use a squirt of mild soapy water to kill
aphids and greenfly on roses and other
garden plants—it prevents them from
flying and subsequently suffocates them.

506 CATERPILLAR CULL

If you have a major caterpillar or slug problem
and need to use chemicals, the least toxic and
therefore most environmentally friendly option
is pyrethrum dust because it kills the lower
species but isn't passed up the food chain.

507 START OFF INSIDE

Instead of protecting tender plants such as cucumber with chemical sprays, start them off inside where you can keep an eye on them until they are hardy enough to withstand garden pests outside.

508 MAKE THE DUST FLY

Stop slugs and snails from munching their way through your favorite plants with sawdust. It dries them out, effectively paralyzing them by preventing them from creating their slimy trail, which allows them to move.

509 DIG A POND

If you have space, creating a pond or water feature in your garden is one of the best steps you can take to promote wildlife. Encouraging frogs and toads will mean you don't have to use slug pellets as they'll feast on your garden pests.

510 WORM AWAY SLUGS

If you have a slug problem but don't want to cover your garden with poisonous slug pellets, why not try natural methods instead? Buy a packet of nematodes. These are small worms that naturally parasitize the slugs and won't harm the rest of your garden.

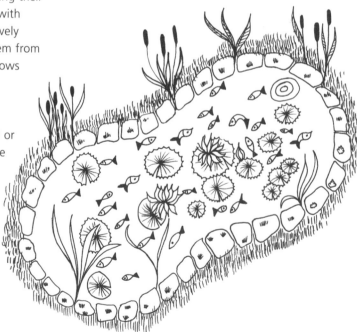

511 WALK ON EGGSHELLS

Instead of using slug pellets, sprinkle eggshells and lemon peel around susceptible plants to deter slugs and snails—they are repelled by the smell of lemon and can't maneuver themselves over eggshells.

512 GO FRENCH

The problem with pesticides is that they are toxic to desirable wildlife as well as the ones you're trying to get rid of. Also, they enter the food, air, earth, and water systems so we consume them without being aware of the implications. Plant marigolds throughout your garden—they work particularly well against tomato pests. Japanese beetles are repelled by rue, while tansy will repel cucumber beetles.

513 EARLY BIRD CATCHES THE WORM

Birds are much more efficient than people at killing bugs, so for pest control, encourage birds into your garden with a bird cone or nut hanger. Woodpeckers, warblers, finches, jays, robins, grackles, sparrows, cedar waxwings, starlings, and many other birds will consume thousands of insects every day.

514 MAKE ORGANIC PESTICIDE

For a totally organic pesticide, stand a large handful of tobacco leaves in about 8 pints of warm water for 24 hours, then use as a spray on leaves to repel insects. But beware—this water is poisonous to humans as well.

515 COZY COMPANION

To encourage natural predators to munch away your garden pests so you don't have to use pesticide, consult your local garden society about local companion planting. The idea is that most plants have favorite "neighbors" that help to prevent disease.

516 JUMP ON THE DERRIS WHEEL

If your garden is really overrun with pests and you need to use a pesticide, choose derris-based. This is a natural pesticide made from tropical plants (but be aware that it will kill all insects, not just the ones you don't want around). Its active ingredient is rotenone, a naturally occurring chemical with insecticidal, spider-killing and fish-killing properties. It is used for insect control and for lice and ticks on pets.

517 PUSH AWAY PESTS

The smell of camomile deters most small flies. Make your own pesticide by infusing camomile flowers in hot water for ten minutes. Spray on plants to prevent pests alighting.

518 DUST CAREFULLY

Sulfur (in dust or liquid form) controls mildew on roses and other flowers and vegetables, and although it's safe for animals, it can be fatally poisonous to fish, so be very careful when using it around water.

519 WARD OFF PESTS WITH ONION

To stop harmful insects taking hold in your pesticide-free garden, plant onion plants, which will repel the larvae of insects and stop them reproducing.

520 PLANT FOR THE BIRDS

Some plant species are known to attract birds into your garden and so reduce pests; pin cherry, white flowering dogwood, honeysuckle, holly, white pine, Russian olive, sunflowers, and marigolds are all good choices.

521 NET A GOOD CROP

Fine netting such as cheesecloth placed over flower and vegetable beds will protect seedlings from chewing insects, keep cats and birds away, and prevent flying insects from laying eggs.

522 GROW SOME GARLIC

Growing garlic near your roses is a great way to protect them from greenfly, who can't bear the smell and won't come anywhere near.

523 PUSS IN FRUITS

Commercial cat deterrent may be harmful to garden birds. Cats don't like the smell of citrus, so instead of spraying your garden with cat deterrent, use essential oil repellents, which are totally natural.

524 GET PRICKLY

To deter ground mammals like rabbits around your tender spring crops, sprinkle dried holly leaves. The holly spikes will hurt their feet and discourage them from approaching. The leaves will biodegrade over time.

525 SOAP AWAY PESTS

For a chemical pest remover with low toxicity, try insecticidal soap. It can be bought from most hardware stores, and helps remove pests without leaving toxic resins on plants.

526 COLLAR YOUR PLANTS

Stop hatching larvae from burrowing into the soil surrounding your plants by using "collars" made of stiff paper. Cut a piece 1 foot by 1 foot and fit it snugly around the base of the plant on top of the soil. Use a paper clip to hold it in place.

527 CHOOSE NONTOXIC DUST

Diatomaceous earth (also known as DE, diatomite, or diahydro) is a highly porous dust made from a naturally occurring, chalk-like sedimentary rock. It consists of fossilized remains of diatoms, a type of hard-shelled algae. DE controls pests by causing dehydration and death. It is a dangerous dust and should be used with care, and not inhaled. Make sure it's not the crystalline or chemically manufactured variety you're buying.

business help

528 GLOVE UP SAFELY

If latex gloves are being used in your place of work, make it plain, non-PVC versions. Avoid powdered gloves or those containing vinyl—they can release poisons when incinerated.

529 BE A TELECOMMUTER

To cut down on pollution caused by your daily commute to work, investigate in the possibility of telecommuting one or two days a week by working from home or a local office. Email and video-conferencing from a home webcam makes this easier than ever before.

530 OUTSOURCE CAREFULLY

Many offices outsource their cleaning and maintenance. Make sure the contractor your company chooses is taking steps to protect the environment by minimizing their use of chemicals in the products they use. If not, ask to consider swapping to a contractor who does.

531 RACK IT UP

Petition your boss to put up a well-lit bike rack close to your office building, if not inside. Having a safe place to store bicycles might encourage more people to bike to and from work.

532 COMMUTE THE GREEN WAY

Walk or ride your bicycle to work instead of taking your car. If you have a long way to travel, trains and buses are better than cars because they cut down your pollution impact.

533 CLEAN GREEN

Encourage your office to implement green cleaning materials and practices. For instance, alternating the use of an electric vacuum cleaner with that of a mechanical carpet sweeper will help cut electricity by half.

534 GET A MICRO MINI

Microfiber mops are a new invention. They have washable cloths, minimizing waste and detergent use, so are great for public areas. Make sure your cleaners at work are using them, or pressure them to change.

535 CHOOSE A GREEN COURIER

If your office sends packages by courier, try to use a bicycle courier rather than cars or motorcycles in an attempt to reduce environmental pollution.

536 AUDIT YOUR ENERGY

Get your employer to do an energy audit or bring in a specialist carbon footprinter to advise managers on where they can make changes that will help the environment. An audit will show you problems that may, when corrected, save money.

537 USE EVERY OTHER LIGHT

Don't complain about those fluorescent office lights—in fact, they're extremely energy efficient. But often they are too heavily used—try to use some portions only, or take out every other strip.

538 DON'T LEAVE IT ON

Make a sign for your office door that says "Last one out, turn off the lights"—often office lights burn right through the night. This will remind cleaners who work in the evening to turn out lights, too.

539 SCREEN YOUR ENERGY USE

There's no need to have your computer screen running if you're at a meeting or off on a coffee or lunch break—turn it off when you're not using it.

540 SHUT DOWN

Encourage your colleagues to shut down their computers when they're not in use unless they've got a low-energy sleep option. This should be done before lunchtime breaks and before going home at the end of the day.

541 MAKE SOME SENSE

Ask your company to swap their water-wasting faucets for sensor varieties, which release water only when you put your hands in front of them. If your company has shower facilities or is installing them, timed sensors can also be used there, which automatically turn off after a few minutes. People will soon adjust to taking shorter showers and conserve water in the process.

542 TAP THE PROBLEM

Faucet aerators reduce the amount of water used by creating an illusion of more water flow. This is particularly important in a large building with public toilets, as these are often hotbeds of water wastage.

543 JUMP IN THE POOL

Some people manage to cut the energy they use to commute to work by car-pooling. When four or five people go in one car rather than separate vehicles, it cuts down on air pollution. In addition, all the cars in the pool will benefit from lower mileage and gasoline expenses.

544 FAN YOURSELF COOL

A ceiling fan in an office is a better choice than air conditioning because it uses much less electricity. It moves the air around the room to produce drafts that are cooling—a healthier choice than artificial cooling.

545 FIX IT

Use reusable fixers like staples, string, paper clips, or nontoxic adhesive instead of adhesive tape, which produces toxins when it's manufactured, can only be used once, and doesn't biodegrade.

546 DRY THE SENSOR WAY

Make sure your office toilets don't have throw-away paper towels. Request sensor dryers that automatically release air if you put your hands in front of the sensor, but doesn't waste energy at other times.

547 JOIN A FRIEND

Commuting is a major cause of traffic pollution and greenhouse gas emissions. According to the Bureau of Transportation, a staggering 89% of workers sit alone in their car on their drive to work. There are many carpool and rideshare websites on the internet and your city government might also facilitate carpool trips.

548 DON'T PICK YOUR SPOTS

Instead of energy-guzzling spotlights, offices should choose smaller power-saving spotlight bulbs that use only 11 watts. This simple change could mean that the office uses a tenth of the energy of previous use.

STAPLES

549 SAY NO TO SOLVENTS

Instead of solvent-based markers and highlighters, use crayons, wax markers, or colored pencils. They will help the air in the office stay free of chemicals.

550 USE LEAD REFILLS

Disposable pencils waste wood as you are never able to use every last bit of it. Opt for a metal refillable pencil instead. It's always sharp and you won't waste any lead because you can use it all.

551 SHARE A PAPER

Instead of everyone in the office buying their own newspaper, leave one copy in the staff room or reception area so that everyone can share the news during lunch and coffee breaks.

552 SORT YOUR ENVELOPES

One of the major turn-offs to reusing envelopes is that you can never lay your hands on one of the right size. Create an envelope sorting system for your used envelopes so you can choose the size you need with little fuss.

553 DON'T DISPOSE OF FILTERS

Instead of disposable paper filters in your office coffee machine, use mesh or permanent cloth. Otherwise it means throwing a filter away every time you've made a cup of coffee.

554 PHONE AGAIN

More than 500 million cellphones are in landfill sites across the globe now, with another 125 million heading to shelves and landfills this year alone! Donate your phone to charity or recycle it with a phone recycling program—most operators now run one.

555 USE A GLASS

Instead of a water dispenser with throw-away paper or plastic cups, keep a supply of glasses nearby and encourage people to use them instead. Alternatively, fill up with your own reusable water bottle.

556 A MUG'S GAME

Instead of relying on disposable styrofoam or plastic cups at work, take in your own ceramic or china mug so you can sip with a free conscience!

557 TAKE A LUNCH BOX

Take your packed lunch to work in a reusable container instead of plastic wrap. A plastic container is useful but metal is a better choice in terms of reducing toxins.

558 DON'T GO FOR THE BURN

If your office has waste that is usually incinerated, remember that this process releases poisonous dioxins. Encourage your bosses to explore alternatives to incineration.

559 USE YOUR WASTE CAREFULLY

Some energy manufacturers now use modern techniques like pyrolysis to produce energy from commercial waste like shredded rubber, sewage sludge, wood wastes, and chicken litter. Make sure your company makes the most of its waste.

560 CHECK THE BOX

Do an office inventory with a column titled "throwing away" and one titled "recycling." Every time you throw something away or recycle it, put a checkmark in the appropriate column. Your aim should be to have more recycling checkmarks.

561 TAKE STOCK

Why not run an office competition to get everyone to make a list of everything they throw away during the course of a day. The idea is to go through this list to see if they could be recycling any of the items.

562 TALK ABOUT IT

Help educate your colleagues about the environment by making a point of telling them when you're making a decision based on green issues. They may start taking your point of view on board.

563 POST A NOTICE

Why not set up an environmental bulletin board to post notices about local environmental meetings, news, and green tips. It will encourage your co-workers to think about their impact on the environment.

564 INVEST ETHICALLY

Encourage your company pension plan to invest ethically—in other words investments made with companies who make it their business not to harm the environment.

home office

565 MAKE GREEN BUSINESS DECISIONS

Take a closer look at the companies you do business with—are they making any effort to be environmentally friendly? Don't take business decisions based on cost and customer service alone—take green issues into account as well.

566 TALK TO THE BOARD

Lobby your company's directors to set up a committee or bring in a specialist to monitor its environmental performance and take steps to minimize its effect on the environment.

567 JOIN A CLUB

Why not encourage your company to join the World Wildlife Fund's international network for reducing one's carbon footprint. They help businesses across the globe to become more environmentally friendly.

568 IONIZE YOUR OFFICE SPACE

Make sure you keep houseplants in your office as they will help counteract the negative radiation effects of electrical equipment in a small space. Or invest in an ionizer that does the same job (preferably a solar-powered one).

569 GET GEEKY WITH YOUR MUSIC

Don't use a separate radio or CD player in your home office. These require batteries and are energy inefficient. Most PCs are now geared up for you to listen to radio, CD, or downloaded music as you work, meaning you're only using one source of power.

570 LIMIT CD BURNING

Instead of buying CDs to transfer data from home to business offices, download your files onto a USB thumb drive or MP3 player (many can act as mini hard drives). You'll save on CD wastage and reduce the environmental pollutants released in their manufacture.

571 DON'T BE A LASER HEAD

Ozone damages the natural balance of the atmosphere's top layers and takes many years to break down. Because laser printers release ozone into the environment, they're best avoided. If you already have one, use it only when really necessary.

572 WORK ASPECTS

Try to position your home office in the sun-facing portion of your house where it will get as much natural light as possible during the day. (This means south-facing in the northern hemisphere.) Open windows to encourage fresh air and good ventilation around the electrical machinery.

573 WORK NEAR A WINDOW

Natural light is known to increase productivity. Place your computer near a window so you can illuminate your monitor by natural rather than artificial light, and you'll save on your electricity bill, too. If the glare is too harsh to see the screen, simply turn your desk so you are facing the window.

574 GET FRESH IN THE OFFICE

When you're thinking about planning your home office, remember that synthetic carpets, petroleum-based paint, and poor ventilation are not just bad for the environmnet but also bad for you. They can all contribute to tiredness and nausea—try to maximize on fresh air and natural fibers.

575 WARM YOUR WATER

Use natural materials and water in your office to maintain humidity. Water droplets in the air will help you to reduce ion depletion caused by electrical equipment. A fresh bowl of warm water on the floor or desk is a good way to do this.

576 HAVE A CUPPA

Drink a cup of tea or coffee by your computer! Steam from your hot drink is absorbed into the air around you and reduces the effects of radiation, restoring the natural balance.

577 FAN YOUR WORKSPACE

If you can't open a window to increase air circulation and reduce radiation effects, install a ceiling fan or use a desk fan to help create gentle air turbulence.

578 BUY RECONDITIONED

Instead of buying a new PC when yours needs replacing, consider investing in a reconditioned machine. Nowadays, many reconditioned computers are just as powerful but you won't be wasting all that plastic and metal casing.

579 USE A DESK LIGHT

In your home office, try to use desk lights instead of overhead lights. The latter use larger bulbs and therefore take up more energy. Remember that it's better for your eyes not to have too much glare on the screen, too.

580 SEND APPLIANCES TO SLEEP

Look for computers and monitors carrying the internationally recognized Energy Star mark—Energy Star is a program to help businesses and individuals protect the environment. While computers are not being used they can "sleep" rather than employ an active desktop or screensaver. The sleep function can reduce energy wastage by 65%.

581 REDUCE YOUR ELECTRICS

All electric equipment releases electromagnetic radiation, thought to be damaging to health if it permeates your home. Use it as little as possible, and reduce the effects by sitting in front of your screen rather than to the side of it. Also sit well back.

582 FLATTEN OUT YOUR VISION

Flat screens use less energy and emit less radiation than standard monitors, so replace your TV and PC screens with flat screens if you can. A smaller screen is usually a better choice as it uses less power to do the same job.

583 SEND A MESSAGE

Send emails instead of relying on the postal service, particularly when you are writing to people in other countries where planes are being used to transport the documents, thereby hiking up the environmental cost.

584 UNPLUG YOUR EQUIPMENT

If your electrical equipment doesn't have a sleep function (this is not the same as standby, which uses energy), make sure you turn it off and unplug it when it's not in use.

585 SLEEP ELECTRICITY-FREE

It's not known how harmful electromagnetic radiation from equipment in your home can be, but it's worth keeping machines away from sleeping areas to reduce possible effects while you sleep.

586 KEEP IT REAL

Wood effect finishes can give off volatile organic compounds (VOCs) that release toxins and pollute the environment. Choose natural solid wood, metal, or glass for your desk at home, and look for low-VOC or no-VOC labeling on paint treatments and varnishes.

587 BULK IT UP

Order supplies for your home office in bulk rather than ordering single items when you run out. That way, your transportation costs will be kept to a minimum because of reduced delivery runs.

588 DO SOME SOLAR SUMS

Choose a solar-powered calculator rather than one that relies on chemical batteries. Calculators require very little power to keep working and most now have solar panels.

589 BE A CLEAN FREAK

Clean and dust your computer regularly to ensure optimal functioning. Don't forget the area behind the screen and where the wires join the base at the back as dirt and dust can easily accumulate here.

590 RECYCLE YOUR INK

Choose a company that recycles printer cartridges—most now run recycling plans by which you can send back your printer cartridges to a central base to be reused and resold. This is essential to cut down on the amount of plastic thrown away.

591 DON'T CHOOSE COMPOSITE

Don't buy a desk made with composite materials that may use PVC in their manufacture, but choose solid wood acquired from a sustainable source, such as those certified by the Forest Stewardship Council.

582 SET UP A SYSTEM

Organize a paper recycling system for your home office, separating cardboard and paper into specific piles to make sure you aren't being tempted to throw it away with your office trash. Or invest in a separate recycling container so you can set aside anything that can be recycled.

583 HIRE A CARPENTER

Instead of spending lots of money on a new desk for your office, invest in some salvaged wood and paying a carpenter to make you one to measure—it will have the added advantage of fitting the space exactly.

584 TRAY A BIT HARDER

When you're choosing trays to organize your paperwork, select those made from metal or wood rather than plastic. Not only does this help limit our reliance on plastic products but it looks more attractive, too.

585 FILE DOWN YOUR METAL

To do your filing without a guilty conscience, buy metal filing cabinets and use recycled paper hanging-file folders (see treecycle.com or look for the recycle logo on stationery supplies). They last for many years—and it is quite easy to buy them secondhand.

586 STICK IT NATURALLY

Choose natural glue made from animal or vegetable products rather than glue made with chemicals. In general, those in sticks or pots are better than those in tubes.

597 STICK ON SOME LABELS

Use stickers to label files and folders instead of plastic tags. A better choice than ready-glued would be gummed versions that you wet on the back (like you do envelopes). Or even better, use a paper clip to attach loose paper as a label.

598 INVEST IN A PEN

Instead of disposable pens that are thrown away after only a short period of use, buy refillable ones. Although they cost more, you can choose a design of pen you really like, knowing that you'll enjoy using it for longer.

599 CORRECT THE GREEN WAY

Aim to use correction tape that covers errors or lifts them off without the use of solvents. When you must use correction fluid, the water-based type made for photocopiers is better than solvent-based, as both the manufacture and disposal of the latter have detrimental effects on the environment. Water-based varieties are better for your health as well.

600 CHOOSE A RECYCLING PROGRAM

Wherever you can, make sure you choose recyclable items and subscribe to programs—usually it will save you money, too. Many companies now have "take back" recycling programs for plastic pen casings, floppy discs, rewritable CDs, and other office materials. The amount of bulk material a company produces makes recycling even more important.

601 RECYCLE YOUR MAT

Many companies offer mouse mats made from recycled plastic. If you have an infra-red mouse, you don't need a mat at all. Some "print your own" companies now also offer mats from recycled materials, so choose it if it's available.

602 PASS IT ON LOCALLY

Before you throw out your computer, check out any local information-technology recycling plans in your area. If you want to donate your machine to be reconditioned for re-sale, your local computer technician or repair store should be able to point you in the right direction.

603 DONATE YOUR PC

When you've finished with your computer, instead of throwing it away, why not donate it to a school, charity, or children's group? Others will benefit from your trash and you won't feel guilty about wastage.

604 TECHNOTRASH YOUR DISKS

Computer disks take an average of 450 years to degrade, and while they do so they can leach damaging oxides into water supplies and so threaten wildlife. Electronic waste includes toxins such as mercury, lead and cadmium—all which can have a hazardous effect on the environment and health. Reuse or send to a recycler. Some recycling centers supply the disks as materials to be re-made into useful objects. They may also take hard drives, motherboards, cords and cables, and other "technotrash."

605 KEY IN YOUR DATA

Use a USB key for your PC instead of a CD or DVD, which is larger and therefore requires more packaging and transportation.

606 SEND BACK YOUR PHONE

Make sure you recycle your cell phone when you've finished with it. Although the metal isn't toxic, LCD screens and batteries will release toxins into the environment as they break down. Your phone supplier should be able to advise you.

paper chain

607 GET AGRO FOR AGRIFIBERS

Try to buy non-wood (wood-free) paper whenever you can. Alternative materials include hemp, kenaf, agricultural residues, and even denim scraps. Many agrifibers yield more pulp per acre than forests or tree farms, and they require fewer pesticides and herbicides.

608 SUPPORT TREES

Buy paper with at least 30% post-consumer recycled content, and encourage your school or workplace to do the same. This way you will support the paper recycling industry and save trees.

609 SORT OUT YOUR LEAVES

Did you know there are nine different grades of paper? Most of the time recycling centers will do the sorting for you but it helps them if, in advance, you can loosely sort your paper into different types like white, newspapers, and glossy magazines and flyers. At the very least divide your paper into black-printed and color-printed.

610 THIN OUT YOUR PAPER

Always buy the thinnest variety of recycled paper for your printer. The thinner the paper, the less paper is used per sheet and so wastage is reduced. Save thick versions for important documents.

611 COPY LESS

Wherever you can, reduce the number of copies of documents you make to the absolute minimum. In your next meeting, could one copy be shared between two people? Can you present a report in a digital form, such as a power point presentation or an email, rather than as a hard copy?

612 KEEP A RECYCLING RECEPTACLE

Make sure your office has a paper recycling container that's emptied regularly. If the receptacle starts overflowing, chances are your colleagues will stop using it.

613 REMEMBER THE SCRAPS

It takes 28% less energy to recycle than to produce paper from scratch, so do recycle all office paper, including envelopes, packaging, magazines, and newspapers.

614 THINK OUTSIDE THE ENVELOPE

Envelopes can be reused many times by pasting labels over the address, then adding your own stamps. Open them with an envelope opener rather than tearing to keep them in good condition for longer.

615 PAPER CUT

Paper comprises over 40% of solid waste in the U.S. (about 72 million tons annually). With little discernable difference in quality, there's no excuse not to buy recycled whenever you can.

616 BACK-UP LISTS

Don't put used envelopes in the recycling receptacle right away—make the best use of them by using the blank back for to-do lists or shopping lists.

617 USE EVERY INCH

Use paper as many times as you can. For example, if you're throwing away a letter that only takes up half a page, cut off the blank piece and use it for lists and scrap paper before you recycle.

618 DROP A FONT SIZE

Dropping a font size when printing your documents—and going for less space between the lines—means you save both ink and paper. This is a good option for documents you are reviewing or using as back-up hard copy rather than sending out.

619 MAKE THE BEST USE OF PAPER

Paper can only be recycled four to six times before it's useless, so make sure you use as much of it as you can. Make it a rule of thumb never to throw away a blank piece of paper.

620 THINK LESS INK

Most modern printers have a draft output option that uses less ink than regular printing. Unless you need to use the extra ink for photos or presentations, click the draft option for everyday printing.

621 CHOOSE A THIN FONT

Choosing a font with thin letters rather than thick, rounded ones will help you save paper because more words will fit onto a page. Next time you're producing a document, experiment with fonts to see which takes up least space.

622 PRINT DOUBLE-SIDED

Make sure you print on both sides of paper. Most printers have double-sided printing functions, or you can do it yourself by printing alternate pages and running the paper through twice.

623 LOOK ONLINE FOR NEWS

Instead of buying a paper-heavy newspaper, read your news online, watch it on television, or subscribe to a telephone text or email messaging service to keep you updated on current issues.

624 GO DIGITAL

Take digital photographs and store them on your PC or in albums online. You can share them with your friends and family without wasting film and paper. If you must have paper albums, keep waste to a minimum and print only those you really want to keep.

beauty matters

625 SPEAK OUT

Why not take a stand by letting brands and manufacturers who consistently over-package their goods know that's the reason you've stopped supporting them. There's nothing like purchasing power to force changes.

626 SAY NO TO SCENT

The majority of perfumes are made entirely from petrochemical products of which the manufacture is very damaging to the environment. They can contain phthalates have been shown to damage the lungs, liver, and kidneys. Instead of buying petrochemical perfume, make your own with a few drops of essential oil in rosewater or carrier oil.

627 TRY TO BLEND IN

Brightly colored cosmetics are likely to contain a lot more chemicals than natural-looking shades. Choose colors sparingly and go for fleshy tones and browns.

628 SMACK YOUR LIPS

Women eat as much as three sticks of lipstick in a lifetime as it works its way from their lips into their mouths. If you choose environmentally friendly versions with natural ingredients you won't ingest toxins.

629 REFILL YOUR PALETTE

When buying makeup, choose refillable palettes—particularly for lip and eye colors or powders. With refillable palettes you'll have less packaging, less wastage and it will be less expensive in the long run.

630 READ THE LABEL

Don't take "natural" for granted—read labels and lists of ingredients to spot synthetics. In Europe and the USA, a product can call itself natural even if only 1% of its ingredients fall into that category. Make sure you're not being taken in by something claiming to be natural when it's not. Look for products that say they are phthalate-free and any seals that claim it is certified organic.

631 THE NATURAL LOOK

Instead of wearing cosmetic products every day, go for a more expensive but greener organic brand and wear less of it. You'll be doing your skin as well as the natural world a favor.

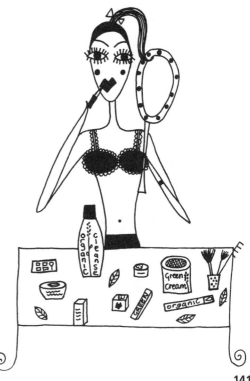

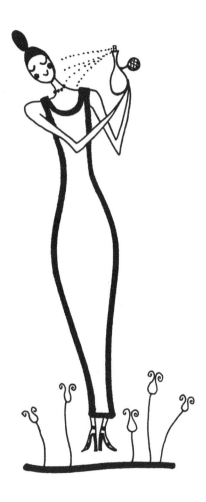

632 SMELL A RAT?

Don't spray yourself with a cloud of poison. 95% of chemicals used in fragrances today are synthetic compounds, including some toxins capable of causing serious health problems. Limit perfumes to special occasions.

633 WAX OR WANE?

Look for natural waxes in mascaras and foundation, like beeswax and carnauba, rather than their manufactured counterparts. These will be easier on your face as well as on the environment.

634 UNSCENTED IS BEST

If you're using so-called "unscented" products, make sure they don't contain a whole array of products to mask scents instead of actually having had nothing added. Check the ingredients to be sure.

635 GET GREEN

Go green in more ways than one by washing your hair in green tea, thought to have natural antibacterial properties that will help reduce scalp sensitivity and will cut down on dandruff.

636 GO NUTS FOR SOAP

If you want a totally natural and biodegradable alternative to soap, grind up some soap nuts and use the powder as a general-purpose soap.

637 LIQUID ASSETS

Plastic soap dispensers are a great choice when it comes to hygiene but bad in terms of packaging. Make your own liquid soap by putting a bar of soap in boiling water and using the liquid to top up your existing applicators.

638 CARE FOR SKIN NATURALLY

Your skin absorbs up to 60% of the products you put on it, and these products can build up over time, so choosing products that are as natural as possible is the sensible choice.

639 WHAT'S IN IT?

Don't be fooled by cosmetic products claiming to be natural. Check the ingredients for the Latin names of plants and for the word "fragrance," which is often code for chemical copies of natural products.

640 MAKE YOUR OWN SOAP

For an ecologically-friendly alternative to chemical-ridden multisurface cleaner, mix ½ cup pure soap with 1 gallon hot water and ¼ cup lemon juice. For a stronger cleaner, double the amounts of soap and lemon juice.

641 MIX YOUR OWN SMELLS

Many bath oils that claim to contain natural products actually contain chemical compounds that have been designed to mimic the smell of natural herbs and fragrances. Instead of wasting your money on artificial smells, why not mix your own with essential oils?

642 GET DARK GLASSES

If you're storing essential oils for use around your home (to replace chemical cleaners or maybe to create your own bathtime fragrance), make sure you keep them in a cool, dark place and in dark glass bottles (rather than plastic containers). The dark glass protects the oil from sunlight and so helps preserve the oil's natural properties.

643 GET OLIVE SKIN

Don't forget olive oil isn't just a staple for your kitchen cupboard—it's also a great choice for moisturizing skin. You can use it as a moisturizing hair mask without having to rely on chemical products with lots of packaging.

644 BODY BEAUTIFUL

When you're choosing body products to use in the bathtub or shower, go for plant-based rather than petroleum-based products because they are more natural and require a lot less manufacture.

645 SALT OF THE EARTH

Instead of foaming bath oils and bubble bath that can contain chemicals like sodium laureth sulphate, choose bath salts to help you relax and unwind when you lie back in the tub.

646 OIL IN MOISTURE

Instead of moisturizer filled with the latest chemical products, use natural oils. Almond oil is a great favorite for sensitive areas, or use hemp or flax oil for hands.

647 GO MINIMAL FOR INGREDIENTS

When it comes to products for your body, how green they are is often directly linked to the number of ingredients. In general, those with fewer ingredients are the better choice, unless it's a long list of essential oils or natural products.

648 VEGGIE ROOTS

Next time you get your roots touched up at the hairdresser, ask for vegetable-based dye rather than chemical alternatives. Not only is it better for the environment, it's also better for your health as you won't absorb potential toxins.

649 PUMP THE ACTION

Wherever you can, choose pump action sprays for beauty products like hairspray and leave-in conditioner rather than aerosol cans. Most products come in alternative packaging nowadays so there's really no excuse to buy an aerosol.

650 STRONG ARM YOUR AEROSOL

Use deodorant crystal or a roll-on rather than an aerosol can—it contributes to air pollution as particles enter the air. Aerosols are also hard to manufacture, requiring lots of energy and producing potential toxins.

651 HALVE YOUR AMOUNTS

Most people use far more shampoo and conditioner than they need. Why not halve your shampoo and conditioner for a week and see if you can tell the difference—chances are that your hair will be just as shiny.

652 RAZOR YOUR RUBBISH

Instead of buying disposable razors and throwing them away after one or two uses, get a metal razor with refillable blades to cut down on the volume of waste leaving your bathroom door.

653 DON'T BE A SQUIRT

Don't squirt out the shaving foam every time you want to de-fuzz—aerosol canisters are environmentally unfriendly. Choose soap instead, or, if you find soap too drying, small amounts of moisturizer do a great job, too.

146

clothing

654 GET A SHOESHINE

Don't throw away your shoes. If they're still in good condition you can give them to charity shops so they can be reused. If they're not wearable, try separating the different materials like fabric, leather, or wood.

655 A RAYON OF LIGHT

Rayon is a great choice for clothes because it's made from trees and plants and therefore involves less of an intensive manufacturing process than some man-made materials.

656 IRON OUT THE KINKS

Many crease- or iron-resistant fabrics have been treated with formaldehyde, poisonous to many living things, and a carcinogen and allergen. Avoid buying non-iron items.

657 SOLE SISTER

Choose shoes with wooden soles rather than plastic, which is harder to manufacture. Wooden soles will last longer so you won't need to replace them so often.

658 DON'T TREAT YOURSELF

If you're buying leather bags and shoes, choose untreated leather or those dyed using vegetable dyes rather than chemicals. Sometimes leather treatment agents can be toxic to natural life.

659 BAG A FRESH DRAWER

Instead of fabric softener, which contains a host of unwanted chemicals, use aromatherapy bags in drawers to freshen clothes up and make them smell sweet and fresh. If you find that lavender is too strong, try dried sage, thyme, or marjoram instead.

660 BE A COTTON TOP

Despite being a natural product, cotton is not actually that environmentally friendly because the plants are treated with so many pesticides and fertilizers. Make sure you always choose organic cotton.

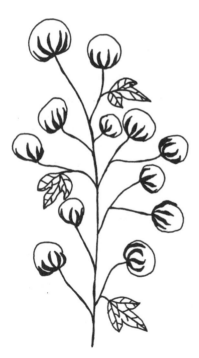

661 WHITE AS A SHEET

Always try to buy unbleached cotton, which is a much better environmental choice than the pure white varieties. If you can't find unbleached, choose those bleached with hydrogen peroxide—they are marginally greener than chlorine bleaches.

662 HEMP IT UNDER

Hemp is a great natural alternative to cotton, especially for underwear, but you can also get hemp outerwear, fitness clothes, footwear, homewares, and linens. The plants are fast-growing and hardy, so don't need pesticides or fertilizers. Hemp is also ideal for sustainable organic farm systems. Be wary of Chinese hemp, which is often processed with chemical acid.

663 QUALITY OVER QUANTITY

Instead of buying cheap, mass-produced clothes that will have to be thrown away at the end of the season, try to invest in as many high-quality pieces as you can. You'll need fewer of them and they will last longer.

664 GO VEGGIE

Look for vegetable rather than
chemical dyes in fabric. Vegetable
dyes are squeezed from pure
vegetable sources, making them
a more natural, non-polluting
choice, and at the same time
completely sustainable.

665 SILKY SMOOTH

Choose your silk carefully as
many chemicals are used
during the manufacture of silk.
Make sure you purchase your
silk from ethical and responsible
suppliers who can vouch for
the production process.

666 SWAP YOUR CLOTHES

Don't throw old clothes away.
Get into the reusing habit by
organizing clothes-swapping
parties with a few friends. Items
no one wants can be taken to a
charity shop or thrift store. There
are often good designer pieces
available from secondhand stores.

667 PLAYING DESIGNER

Don't throw clothes away between
seasons or when they get a small hole
or tear. Invest in a sewing machine and
use it to customize clothes you would
otherwise throw away.

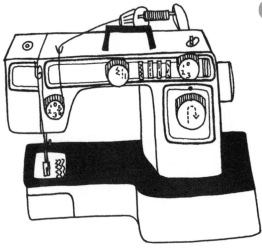

668 PURE POWER

When choosing wool products, the best
label to go for is organic 100% pure new
wool, so you can be sure it is a totally
natural product. Try to find those dyed
with natural dyes to keep chemicals used
to an absolute minimum.

669 BE A WOOLLY ONE

If you're buying organic wool, make
sure it comes from a farm that
hasn't used organophosphates. These
are environmental hazards and can
cause allergies.

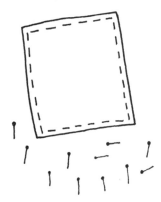

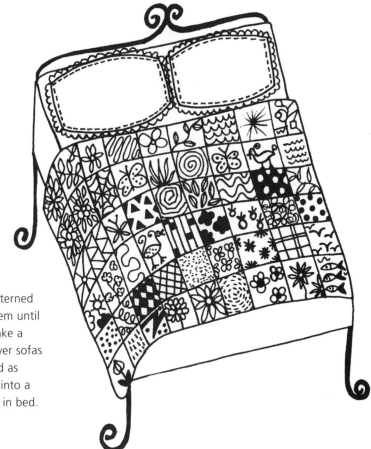

670 PATCH IT UP

Instead of throwing patterned textiles away, collect them until you have enough to make a patchwork throw to cover sofas or armchairs, to be used as a floor rug, or to make into a quilt to keep you warm in bed.

671 YOU CAN BANK ON IT

The average garbage can contains 10% of unwanted household textiles. Textile banks make the best use of your unwanted textiles by recycling them and turning them into other fabrics, often insulating fabrics.

672 BE A TECHNOPHILE

Get creative with materials when you go clothes-shopping. Be on the lookout for the latest techno fabrics, such as PCR (post consumer recycled) or eco-fleece, which is made from recycled plastic bottles.

673 GO RECYCLABLE FOR OUTDOORS

Hard-wearing outdoor clothing often doesn't break down naturally when disposed of, but there are several manufacturers who are making efforts. Patagonia's Capilene 4 garments use Polartec Power Dry fabric, made from 50% recycled polyester fibers and completely recyclable through its Eco-Circle program. Other similar developments have been achieved by Wellman, for their fleece EcoSpun (PET) garments and Unifi's Repreve, which is used in Malden Mills fleeces and Consoltex's Earthwhile outerwear.

food & drink

674 MILES AWAY

Food imported by air is a huge contributor to global warming. According to author and environmentalist Bill McKibben, 75% of the apples sold in New York City come from the West Coast or overseas, even though the state produces far more apples than city residents consume. Wherever you live, try to minimize your food miles by choosing seasonal and local.

675 BE A FARM SHOPPER

Wherever you can, visit local farm shops or farmers' markets for local produce. Not only will it be fresher but you'll be cutting down your environmental costs.

676 FILL A BOTTLE

Join bottle-refilling programs offered by some local stores and farm markets. They will fill up your existing bottles of oil, vinegar, and other kitchen essentials to save you having to buy and throw away glass bottles. Some beauty product companies also operate a refilling option.

677 GET THE LOW DOWN

Provided that you buy locally, fruit, vegetables, and crops require far less energy than meat production. So try eating lower down the food chain. Even non-vegetarians can limit the amount of meat they eat quite easily; for example, by choosing it only every other day.

678 CHOOSE LOCAL FRUIT

Not only does fruit flown in from around the globe have a harsh impact on the environment through fuel emissions, it also needs more protective packaging to keep it in a decent state, so it's a double whammy. Choose less packaged, local produce instead.

679 DON'T THROW AWAY THE WINE

Reduce wine waste with a vacuum cork, so you don't have to throw away surplus wine if you don't finish a bottle. Opened bottles should be used within three days and kept sealed in the refrigerator to slow down the oxidation process. You can also buy special champagne stoppers to help preserve the bubbles.

680 CLOSE TO HOME

Whenever you can, visit a local butcher, fish dealer, and farm market who will supply you with as much fresh, local food as possible. Or get proactive and pressure your local supermarket to set up a small section selling only local food, if they don't do so already.

681 GET LOOSE

Next time you're in the fruit and vegetable sections of your supermarket, put fruit and vegetables into your cart loose rather than automatically reaching for a plastic bag. If you really need one, keep it and reuse next time.

682 THE BEST VEGETABLES

Eating organically grown fruit and vegetables doesn't just reduce the amount of pesticides and fertilizers released into the environment, it's also more healthy—for you, the farmers, and food handlers.

683 GET ORGANIC JUICE

Apples can be sprayed with pesticide up to 35 times before they reach your fruit bowl, so a brief run under running water is not going to make much difference. Buy organic, especially for juice where toxic residues will be concentrated.

684 BRAIN BOX

The greenest way to buy your fruit and vegetables is through an organic vegetable program. Because it's delivered to local areas all at once, transportation costs are minimal.

685 PEEL YOUR FRUIT

If you buy non-organic fruit, make sure you peel it. The peel is often the most nutrient-rich part, but unfortunately it's also the part that holds onto the residue from chemicals.

686 BUY SEASONAL PRODUCE

Next time you reach for strawberries in the middle of winter, think about whether you really need them—the global movement toward food being available all year round leads to massive travel costs and pollution. Try buying foods seasonal to your local climate.

687 PRETTY PRESERVES

Don't be tempted to buy fresh fruit flown in from across the globe in wintertime. Cut down on food miles by buying local fruit when it's in season, and freezing or preserving it to keep you going when it's not.

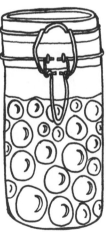
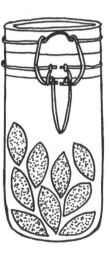

688 GET BUTCHER'S BLOCK

One of the best things you can do to make your meat a green choice is abandon the supermarket and visit a butcher who sources meat locally and is able to tell you the origin of what you're buying. They often have long-established connections with specific farms and will know about the raising of the animals. They keep packaging to a minimum, too.

689 CHECK YOUR INGREDIENTS

If you are buying meat from a supermarket, make sure you check the ingredients list carefully. There should be nothing but meat in it. Anything saying "meat protein" means you're buying heavily processed food.

690 SLOW FOOD MAKES MORE SENSE

Don't spend your money supporting global fast-food chains. They contribute to intensive farming practices in order to produce the large quantities of meat they sell daily. Go to a local restaurant, where you can be sure the meat is responsibly sourced.

691 BUY ADDITIVE-FREE

Organic meat is the best choice, but if you can't find any or you think it is too expensive for your budget, choose free-range, additive-free instead. Often this meat comes from farms undergoing a conversion to organic, so it's basically organic meat at a cheaper price.

692 HAVE A FISH DINNER

When you eat seafood, steer clear of endangered species. In the case of salmon, for example, choose a sustainably fished species, such as wild Alaskan, over farm-raised (which pollutes watersheds) or wild Atlantic (which is at historic lows). Avoid endangered fish like Chilean sea bass and Pacific snapper. If in doubt, check Fish Watch at the NOAA (www.nmfs.noaa.gov).

693 EAT LEAN MEAT

Whenever you can, eat lean meat. Chemicals from animal feed, antibiotics, or fertilizers in grass are stored more in fat than in muscle, accumulating to high levels. Making sure you cut fat off meat could lessen your chances of ingesting it.

684 CHOOSE FREE-RANGE

Never buy eggs that aren't free-range.
Birds in battery cages are often kept in
appalling conditions and without freedom
to roam. (Note that all organic eggs are
free-range, although all free-range eggs
aren't necessarily organic.)

695 BE A HOME COOKER

Home-cook whenever you can. With fresh food, very little or no processing is involved. This minimizes the energy used to get it to your plate and therefore also the cost to the environment.

696 WALK THE LINE

When buying wild fish such as tuna and marlin, make sure you choose fish caught by long lines rather than nets. This ensures that no dolphins or other aquatic species have been harmed to get you your dinner.

697 ABOVE WATER

Where you can, choose fish from one of the few sustainable waters around the world where fish quotas have been carefully controlled for years, meaning they are less overfished than others. Check if the fishery is listed with the National Marine Fisheries Service (www.nmfs. noaa.gov).

698 FARM YOUR FISH

Don't worry about buying farmed fish as long as it's organic—organic fish farming processes are humane and overfeeding of fish is not allowed. Fish are kept in natural river habitats without the use of dyes.

699 A MEATY MATTER

Buy free-range, organically raised meat and poultry products. The animals will have been raised humanely and on untreated feeds, resulting in chemical-free food. You can also be assured that the soil from these farms is treated well, reducing the impact on wildlife habitats.

700 SIP A BREW

You might think you're choosing the healthy option by going for herbal tea, but make sure you choose organic—otherwise the herbs used to make them could have been heavily drenched with pesticides.

701 MILK YOUR LOCAL FARMS

Organic dairy produce is a good choice because you can be sure it's free from antibiotics and pesticide residues. Look for local milk from farms certified by the USDA's National Organic Program (www. ams.usda.gov/NOP)

702 LOOK AT TEA LABELS

Buy tea and coffee with the organic label where you can. If you can't afford organic, choose fair trade, which limits the use of chemicals to ensure a non-toxic work environment for workers.

703 ROOT OUT GM

Around 60 to 70% of processed foods on American shelves contain ingredients derived at least in part from genetically-modified crops, but there is no labeling required by the FDA unless the composition of the food differs substantially from its conventional counerpart. Watch for GM foods hiding in ingredients lists as "modified." And if you want to ensure your food is GM-free, choose organic.

704 PACK IT IN

Make food choices based on the amount of packaging they are presented in. Particularly try to cut down on the amount of plastic involved, because the environmental costs for plastic is sky high. Where possible, choose loose fruits and vegetables from farmer's markets.

706 CHOOSE YOUR CHOCOLATE

There are so many organic products to choose from these days that it's often hard to know which ones to choose. The cocoa plant is one of the most heavily sprayed in the world, so keep chocolate on your organic list. Many good organic brands use cocoa sourced in Central and South America. Make sure, however, that the manufacturer certifies that all of the cocoa they purchase is produced without the use of forced labor.

707 HERB YOUR ENTHUSIASM

Don't buy packaged fresh or dried herbs in the supermarket when you can grow them in your kitchen. They are easy to grow, last much longer than store-bought herbs, and make your kitchen smell good, too. Some supermarkets sell growing herbs for this use.

705 DON'T BE A WHINER

Organic wine is a great choice because it contains fewer sulfur deposits and chemicals, although you'll have to do without a huge variety. Make sure you choose single-estate wines, where you can be more sure of quality.

708 LETTUCE GROW

Don't think that lettuce is impossible to grow if you don't have a garden—it's the perfect crop for windowsills as they prefer sheltered, sunny spots. Simply plant out the seedlings and watch them grow.

709 PACK IN THE PACKAGING

Avoid buying food in plastic containers made of unrecyclable plastic. If possible, choose loose items or go for paper or cardboard packaging instead.

710 DON'T TIE YOURSELF IN KNOTS

Don't tie plastic bags too tight—you'll have to tear them open and then won't be able to reuse them. Instead, use loose knots, or seal with reusable ties if you need it to be airtight.

711 PUT IT UNDER GLASS

Avoid storing food in plastic. Use reusable glass containers to store food in the refrigerator and freezer, but check before you use it in the freezer as not all glass containers can be frozen. Always leave space for food to expand.

712 SAVE ON BULK

In your weekly supermarket trip, select large sizes instead of individual serving sizes. You'll save on packaging and you'll be surprised at how much extra you have left in your wallet.

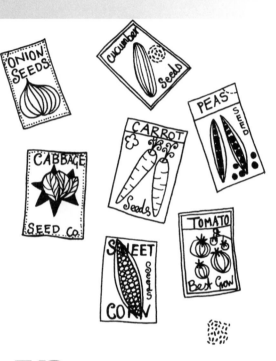

713 GROW YOUR OWN

Instead of buying organic vegetables, grow your own. You don't need a massive vegetable patch—try space-saving ideas like tomatoes and herbs in windowboxes and lettuce on the kitchen windowsill. All it takes is a small grow-bag on your windowsill or a hanging basket and you could have a supply for the whole summer.

714 SUPERSIZE ME

Buy larger packages that have a higher ratio
of content to packaging. Always buying
the largest available, but buying less often,
will not only cut down on the number
of supermarket visits, but also on the
packaging you're buying.

715 GLASS IS CLASS

Instead of buying your milk in plastic bottles (plastics migrate toxins into the food they contact), get glass bottles delivered from your local dairy—they are reused and less energy is used to get it to you. Or choose unbleached cardboard milk cartons.

716 LEAVE IT ALONE

Don't let cling film come into contact with food. Make sure you don't buy cling film made from PVC or vinyl—they are more likely to leach harmful substances into food and are more damaging to the environment.

717 SAY NO TO PLASTIC

If you're going to microwave food, don't do it in a plastic container that might release chemicals into the food when heated. It's best to avoid even those that claim to be microwave safe.

718 REDUCE EMPTY CALORIES

Eat fewer empty calories and you will find you require less food, and therefore less packaging. Most additives in processed foods are chemicals that lack nutritional value so you'll have to eat more of them to get adequate nutrition.

719 SAVE YOUR BREAD

If you find you waste a lot of bread because it goes moldy in your bread box, put a dab of vinegar on a tissue or cloth inside the bread box. The acetic acid in vinegar kills mold, so your bread stays fresher and you'll waste less. Alternatively, buy large amounts but freeze a third or half the loaf.

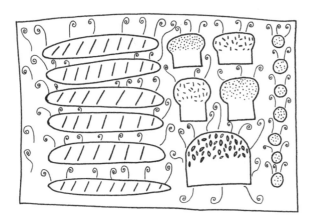

720 PROCESS OF ELIMINATION

Processing food expends many times more energy than the natural product. For example, a 1-pound box of cereal requires nearly seven times as many kilocalories of energy to produce than it provides in nourishment. The greenest choice is to buy as little processed food as possible.

721 MAKE A LITTLE TEA

Don't boil more water than you need for one cup of tea or coffee (but make sure you cover the element completely). The energy wasted boiling a kettle full of water instead of one cup's worth just three times a day could be enough to power one energy-saving light bulb for nine hours.

722 KEEP IT COLD

Instead of running the faucet through until it gets cold every time you want a drink of cold water, keep a covered jug of water in the refrigerator. This way water at the right temperature is always available.

723 SAVE YOUR PEELINGS

Don't throw away fruit and vegetable peelings. If you don't compost, they can make great food for local wildlife. Contact your county environmental-health office for advice on where they can be left to benefit animals without attracting pests.

724 DON'T BE A MUG

If every coffee-drinking American used a refillable instead of disposable mug, it would save close to 7 million pounds of carbon dioxide emissions every day.

725 HANDY HYGIENE

When preparing food, it's unnecessary to run the water throughout preparation to wash your hands. Fill a small bowl with water at the beginning and use as you need it.

726 SUPPORT WILD BIRDS

Herbicides used on crops are damaging wild bird populations by taking away the birds' natural habitats and directly affecting feeding and nesting. Choosing organic is the only way to support wild birds.

727 CHEW IT UP

Choose mastic-based gum for your chewing habit—normal gum takes years to biodegrade and can cause problems for wildlife because of its stickiness. Mastic gum is made from the resin of the Aegean mastic tree and is 100% natural. It is available in gum and capsule form from health food stores.

health & hygiene

728 PLAY BALL

When your running shoes are worn beyond use, don't throw them away. Because of their high rubber content and the fact that rubber is easily recyclable, old sneakers are now being used to make new sports surfaces. Nike is one brand that operates this function by producing it's Nike Grind material.

729 A WEIGHTY MATTER

Ten treadmills in the average gym use the same amount of electricity in a day that it would take to run your hairdryer non-stop for a year. Stick to weights and non-electric machines like spinning bikes.

730 DON'T TEE OFF AT RANDOM

Be discerning about your choice of golf course—choose one that tries to reduce or eliminate the use of poisonous pesticides on greens and fairways by using nontoxic alternatives.

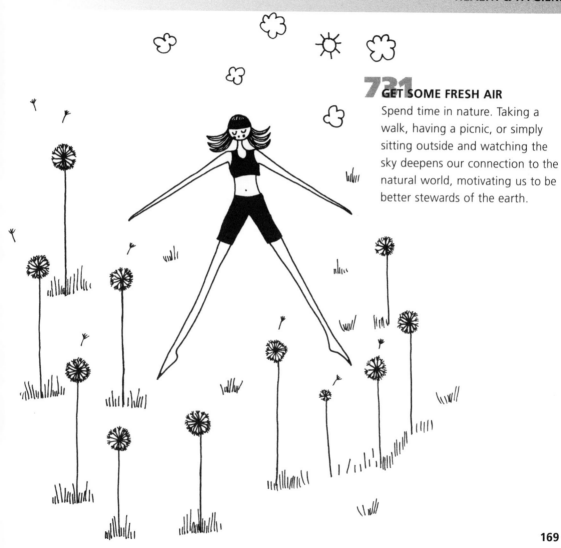

731 GET SOME FRESH AIR

Spend time in nature. Taking a walk, having a picnic, or simply sitting outside and watching the sky deepens our connection to the natural world, motivating us to be better stewards of the earth.

169

732 GO NATURAL

Choose natural fabrics to exercise in rather than highly engineered versions that require lots of energy to produce. If you must buy the latest hi-tech fabrics, make sure you buy quality so you won't have to replace them soon.

733 GET OUTSIDE

Instead of heading for the bright lights of the gym next time you work out, take a step into the fresh air. Running, walking, and working out outdoors have little effect on the environment.

734 WRAP IT UP

When it comes to that time of the month, it's difficult to think of being green, but simple steps can be taken. Purchasing sanitary napkins that are not individually wrapped are a good start to reducing your environmental impact.

735 DON'T APPLY

When choosing tampons, avoid unnecessary packaging like plastic applicators. Disposable plastic is a bad environmental choice. If you have to use disposable tampons, those you apply yourself are best.

736 WHAT A WASTE

Instead of using sanitary napkins that are thrown away after a few hours, consider changing to reusable sanitary towels that can be washed. This will cut down your monthly waste by a considerable amount. Organic cotton tampons without applicators are another green choice as they won't have any of the chlorine, dioxins, synthetic chemicals, or fragrances of ordinary tampons.

737 DON'T FLUSH YOUR FLOATERS

Don't flush your used tampons down the toilet. Wrap them in a small amount of toilet roll and dispose of in the waste can to avoid your personal waste finding its way into public water systems.

738 CUP YOUR FLOW

The most environmentally friendly option when you've got your period is the use of a silicone menstrual cup that is available commercially. It is worn internally like a tampon but collects menstrual fluid rather than absorbing it. The fluid can be flushed away and the cup washed and reused.

739 HEAL YOURSELF WITH TEA TREE

Tea tree oil is a great alternative to chemical healing ointments and balms. A natural antiseptic, it's great in emergencies for cuts and grazes as well as for cleaning up after animals (or children) who have not been housetrained.

740 BE CHOOSY ABOUT FILLINGS

Make sure your dentist isn't using mercury-based fillings or ones that contain heavy metal ions. Go for the safer option of gold or ceramic fillings. If you have mercury fillings removed, make sure they are disposed of with care so they don't poison waterways.

741 SAY ALOE TO STINGS

Don't invest in chemical creams for stings and bruises when natural products will do just as well to help you heal quickly. Aloe vera is a great soothing product that can be used on itchy skin. It also helps bites and stings to heal and can ease the pain of burns. Aloe vera produces around six different antiseptics, which can kill mold, bacteria, and fungus.

742 BLOW YOUR NOSE ON COTTON

Use cotton handkerchiefs that can be washed after use instead of disposable tissues. This will not only help save trees, but the cotton will be softer on your nose.

743 ARNICA AWAY WOUNDS

Help your wounds heal with arnica instead of highly packaged and produced creams designed to do the same job. Arnica soothes muscle aches, reduces inflammation, reduces bruising, and is great for skin problems such as acne and insect bites. It should not be used on broken skin or by those who suffer from skin sensitivity.

744 PHARM AROUND

Choose pharmaceutical companies who invest in green chemistry, whereby chemists are encouraged to develop environmentally friendly products alongside their normal product lines. Ask them about their green programs and choose accordingly.

745 QUESTION TIME

Pharmaceutical companies have historically been very bad at releasing damaging compounds. Don't be afraid to ask your pharmaceutical company what they are doing to reduce the release of solvents and other poisons into the environment.

746 SAY NO TO CHLORINE

Look for pharmaceutical products using the new techno ingredient of supercritical carbon dioxide as solvents for medicines, instead of chlorine and fluorine compounds, which have historically been used to carry other materials in solution.

747 GET GOOD GLASS

Whenever you can, opt to buy varieties of medicines stored in glass rather than plastic bottles. Recycling a glass bottle can save enough energy to light a 100-watt bulb for four hours.

748 BANDAGE IT UP

When you're choosing bandages and band-aids for your first-aid kit, choose those with solvent-free adhesives. They are kinder to skin and you can be sure that the environment has not been harmed during their manufacture.

749 SMALL STEPS IN THE RIGHT DIRECTION

Some smaller pharmaceutical companies are promoting environmental stewardship, investigating new ways to move the industry forward with respect for the environment. Choose them for your medicines.

750 CHOOSE ORGANIC MEDS

Wherever possible, pick up organic varieties of medicines. The manufacturers would have put some thought into the production process and packaging to minimize effects on the environment.

751 WELL-ORIENTED

If you use Chinese medicine, ask your doctor to ensure that none of the remedies you are prescribed are sourced from endangered species like tigers and turtles. Most doctors are willing to find a plant alternative.

752 DON'T CHUCK IT OUT

Don't throw old medicines down the toilet or in the garbage as they can harm the environment. It's a better idea to take out-of-date medicines back to your local pharmacy or hospital where they can be properly disposed of.

753 PUT SOME PRESSURE ON

Hospitals are among the worst offenders when it comes to producing waste. Put some pressure on your local hospital to do a waste count, and then encourage them to come up with ways to minimize their garbage.

754 NO SMOKE WITHOUT A FIRE

Simply don't smoke. Smoking releases toxins into the environment, heats up the local atmosphere, and creates an astounding amount of nondegradable waste every year. Above all, it also causes serious health problems, requiring energy-using medical intervention.

755 SLEEP NATURALLY

Don't reach for the sleeping pills next time you're having trouble dropping off—not only can you become reliant on using them to get to sleep, but many also give you an unpleasant hangover feeling the next day. Try natural sleep enhancers like lavender essential oil and camomile tea.

756 GO PVC-FREE

PVC-free intravenous and blood bags are widely available, as are alternatives for disposable PVC gloves. Likewise, PVC-free or DEHP-free tubing is on the market for most medical applications. Encourage your local hospital not to use PVC if it can be avoided.

757 NO PUBLIC PVC

Construction materials, furnishings, and furniture products account for approximately 75% of all PVC use. As PVC damages the environment by both its manufacture and its disposal, try and encourage local hospitals, schools, and other public organizations to minimize their use of it.

758 CHOOSE A SAFER OPTION

Glutaraldehyde disinfectants, which can cause asthma and skin problems as well as poison the environment, are often used by hospitals because they are economical. They are, however, harmful if inhaled or swallowed and can cause irritation to the eyes and skin. The disinfectant is often used to kill viruses on surgical instruments that are too delicate to be heat-treated. If you are worried you are exposed, see the Center for Disease Control, www.cdc.gov/niosh/.

759 GO LARGE FOR TOOTHPASTE

Buy your toothpaste in the largest tube size possible to maximize the ratio of toothpaste to packaging, but avoid the pump action plastic bottles. They are heavy on packaging and difficult to recycle.

760 GET VEGGIE TEETH

If you want to be even greener when it comes to your dental hygiene, choose a toothpaste based on vegetable products rather than the more common chemically manufactured versions. You'll need less for each application, too.

761 WEAR GLASSES WITH PRIDE

Contact lenses are great when it comes to practicality, but the chemicals used for hard lenses and the amount of packaging for disposables make them a bad environmental choice. Save them for sports and special occasions, and wear glasses at other times.

762 DON'T BE CORNFLOWER BLUE

Talcum powder can pollute the atmosphere and may be carcinogenic if breathed in. It has also been found to have dangerous similarities to asbestos. An ingredient in home and garden pesticides and flea and tick powders, talc is used in smaller quantities in deodorants, chalk, crayons, textiles, soap, insulating materials, and paint. If you really need to use powder, remember that cornstarch is a natural and nontoxic alternative. There are also talc-free baby powders you can use.

763 NOW WASH YOUR HANDS

Encourage your doctor and other healthcare professionals to use alcohol-based hand-rub gels to stop the spread of germs, rather than antimicrobial products.

planning for the future

764 DON'T BE SHY

One of the best things you can do to help the environment is to talk about your green decisions—letting people know they can do something small to help the environment is a major step in changing behavior. The more you enlighten people to the green options there are, the more chance of change.

765 MAKE A PLAN

Don't try to change your life dramatically all in one go—chances are you'll be back where you started before long. Be realistic about making green changes and incorporate them gradually into your lifestyle.

766 BE ETHICAL ABOUT INVESTMENTS

There are many ways to ensure your money doesn't go toward supporting unethical companies. Choose one with humanist, animal welfare, and environmental credentials to ensure you're helping all round.

767 BORROW ETHICALLY

Ensure you live guilt-free in your home by using an ethical mortgage company. They will make sure your money isn't used to support businesses that harm the environment or contribute to habitat loss.

768 GO NATURALLY

Why not make eco-friendly plans for after your death by choosing to be buried in a biodegradable coffin. Coffins made from recycled cardboard will allow your body to decompose naturally, meaning you're giving something back to nature.

769 VISIT THE LIBRARY

To make real changes to your life, you need to learn about the environment and why change is so vital. Visit your local library for a book on global warming or search the internet.

770 LEAVE A LEGACY

You can leave money to environmental causes in your will to help preserve the earth and wildlife habitats for future generations. Charity donations can be tax-free as well.

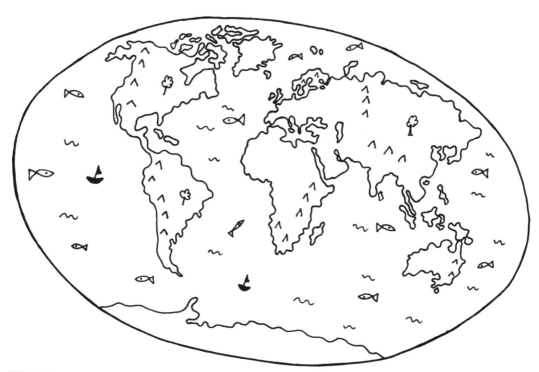

771 GO THE GREEN WAY

Make your last action on earth
a green one by choosing an eco-burial.
Many localities now have forest burial sites
where a tree is planted on each plot.

shopping

772 KNOW YOUR INGREDIENTS

When choosing organic produce, read the labels properly. "100% organic" means it contains only organic ingredients, "organic" means at least 95% is organic and "made with organic ingredients" means only 70%.

773 PAY BY CARD

If you're looking to buy birthday, Christmas, or other greeting cards, explore charity and recycled cards. Some card companies have relationships with organizations such as Unicef or the WWF, so your purchases can help others and the planet.

774 SEND AN E-CARD

Send an e-card instead of buying cards and envelopes made from paper and then relying on road or air transport for them to be delivered. It's cheaper, easier, and much better for the environment.

775 BUY RIGHT

If you're buying gifts for new or expecting parents, expose them to the wide array of alternatives, including sleepers made from organic cotton, toys made from non-dyed wood, and baby soaps made without synthetic ingredients.

776 DON'T BUY CORAL

Consider carefully the coral objects you buy for your coffee table. Find out from which country the coral has been taken and whether or not that country has a management plan to insure the harvest was legal and sustainable.

777 HELP NATURAL RESOURCES

Don't decorate your home with products that come from endangered and threatened plant and animal species. If you're unsure about the material, always ask, and don't support businesses that denude natural resources or threaten animals.

778 GIVE A GLOBAL GIFT

Why not join a global gift program next Christmas—you can buy anything from a ranger kit for local rainforest workers in Borneo to a bicycle to help environmental officers in Tanzania. Organizations like WWF have plenty of global gift ideas.

779 GET ADOPTIVE

If you're thinking of buying a present for an animal-loving friend, don't forget you can adopt an animal for them in many of the world's endangered habitats. Popular choices include tigers, pandas, and orangutans.

780 CLEAN UP YOUR ACT

If you're buying gold jewelry, make sure your gold isn't "dirty." The No Dirty Gold campaign (www.nodirtygold.org) makes sure the jewelry you buy hasn't been produced at the expense of communities, workers or the environment.

781 ALL THAT GLITTERS

The gold produced for a single 18-karat gold ring leaves in its wake 18 tons of mine waste. Every year the smelting industry adds more than 140 million tons of sulfur dioxide to the atmosphere, representing 13% of global emissions. Think carefully before you buy.

782 GO FOR VINTAGE

Instead of choosing new gold for your necklace or wedding ring, buy recycled or vintage gold. You can also get an old gold piece melted down to create a new ring. About one-third of the gold in use or storage today comes from scrap or recycled sources.

783 GREEN GEMS

Choose a gem supplier who has strict environmental and labor standards, such as making sure that laborers are fairly treated and that a mine site is restored to its original condition once mining has been completed.

784 LOOK AT THE LABEL

Read labels carefully and avoid anything containing triclosan or other antimicrobial agents—from soaps, toothpaste, cosmetics, and sponges, to carpets, plastic kitchenware, and even toys.

785 GO BIG

If you have to buy water in plastic bottles, remember that small bottles are heavier on packaging than large ones. Jumbo bottles are the best option of all.

786 DON'T CUT YOUR FLOWERS

Don't buy mass-produced cut flowers, which are grown quickly and using chemicals. Choose organic flowers instead—they don't strip the earth of its natural goodness.

787 GET PLANTED

If possible, buy plants instead of cut flowers to give to your family and friends. Plants continue growing, whereas flowers will be thrown away and wasted after just a few days or weeks.

788 GIVE SOMEONE A TREE

Next time you have to fork out for a birthday present, why not buy a tree instead of the latest toiletries? If the recipient doesn't have space for a tree, there are several global organizations who will organize tree planting in endangered rainforests.

789 KEEP IT REAL

Instead of buying a disposable camera, go for the real thing, even if you don't take that many pictures. Over the course of a year, you will make considerable savings and you'll be doing your part to reduce waste as well.

790 WALK IT OUT

Instead of driving to the supermarket, try walking to your local stores. You will be saving on air pollution by cutting down on gas, you'll be supporting your local economy, and your own health will benefit, too. This might not be practical if you're going to carry heavy shopping, but is a healthy and green choice if you're mailing a letter or going out for a paper.

791 BAG IT

Plastic bags are major environmental no-nos. Keep a stash of reusable cloth or plastic bags in your car so you won't forget to take them along when you go shopping.

792 TIE THE ECO-KNOT

If you're planning a wedding, party, or other special celebration, some companies now offer green alternatives for your special day, such as recycled party tents and flooring as well as reduced energy usage. Investigate local companies who do this.

793 CULL A JOURNEY

The average car emits twice its weight in greenhouse gas carbon dioxide each year. Cut out just one trip a week to make a difference to the amount of exhaust fumes you release—over a year this will add up to quite a lot.

794 SWAP A MAG

Instead of buying several magazines every month, make a deal with your friends to buy one title each and then swap to take a stand against paper waste. This is a way to save yourself some money as well as paper. Or alternate the magazines you buy, limiting yourself to one a month.

795 KEEP THEM IN THE KNOW

Make choices about the food and other goods you buy based on packaging and content, and let your retailer know you're doing so. There's nothing like the prospect of losing money to effect change!

796 TAKE YOUR OWN

Instead of reaching for a plastic bag when you're shopping for fruit and vegetables, take your own brown paper bags or reuse plastic bags so you don't contribute to more plastic waste than you need to.

797 BAG A GREEN DEAL

If you want to invest in a reusable shopping bag to cut down your reliance on disposable plastic bags, choose a sturdy version made from hemp or jute. This will last a lifetime and is more energy-efficient to produce than plastic versions.

tourism

798 BE AN INFREQUENT FLYER

Air transport is now the fastest growing source of carbon dioxide emitted into the Earth's atmosphere. Instead of flying long-distance for your family vacation this year, why not explore your own state?

799 KEEP IT SHORT

Air travel is one of the largest causes of greenhouse gas emissions, so keep it short if you can. Consider going short-haul rather than long-haul for vacations.

800 CLEAN A REEF

Why not do some good on your next vacation by volunteering to clean up a coral reef. You'll spend an afternoon, day, or even a week enjoying the beauty of one of the world's most amazing treasures while helping to preserve it for future generations.

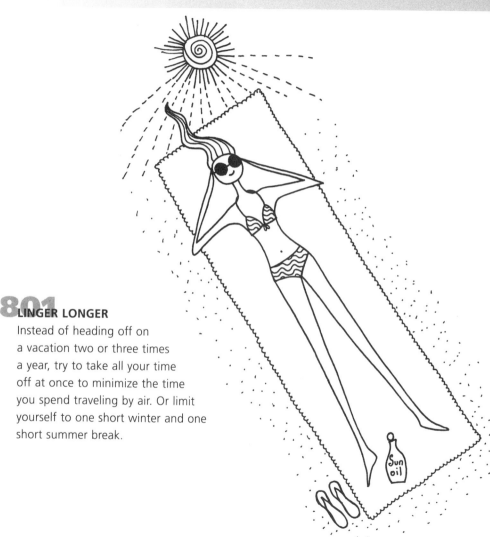

801 LINGER LONGER

Instead of heading off on
a vacation two or three times
a year, try to take all your time
off at once to minimize the time
you spend traveling by air. Or limit
yourself to one short winter and one
short summer break.

802 DON'T STRAY OFF THE PATH

If you go on an excursion, stick to footpaths and marked paths. If you don't, you could trample or squash important wildlife species like beetles, plants, and mushrooms.

803 ADD LOCAL COLOR

Hire local guides when visiting coral reef ecosystems. Not only will you learn about the local resources, but you will be protecting the future of the reef by supporting a non-consumptive economy around the reef.

804 SAVE THE TURTLES

In the Caribbean, endangered leatherback turtles are often the victims of poaching. Visitors can donate money to help save them, or even volunteer for anti-poaching watches as part of the vacation experience.

805 STAY AWAY FROM SOUVENIRS

Although it may be tempting to bring something back from your vacation, don't be tempted to bring back wildlife souvenirs. This will only encourage locals to plunder natural resources.

806 LET NATURE BE

Don't be tempted to take a piece of nature with you. Taking pebbles from beaches, cuttings from trees or plants, or anything from nature reserves will damage wildlife habitats.

807 THROW IN THE TOWEL

When you next stay in a hotel or guest house, you can help them save water by cutting laundry costs. Ask them not to change your towels every day—every three days should be fine.

808 GIVE GENEROUSLY

Support local charities when you next go on vacation by giving a donation through your tour operator or donating your leftover currency through your hotel or travel agent. Most have a list of official local charities.

809 OFF-PISTE ... OFF LIMITS

Take advice from your local ski guide before you ski or snowboard off-piste. In some areas, this can cause severe damage to the natural environment as well as increase the risk of avalanches.

810 SIDESTEPPING THE SNOW

Cross-country skiing is a greener choice for your next winter break than downhill skiing or snowboarding because it requires very little extra equipment or machinery, which means a smaller environmental impact.

811 USE THE SUN'S POWER

Instead of taking a battery-powered radio or CD player on vacation with you, take a wind-up or solar radio with you so you can listen to music or the radio with a guilt-free conscience.

812 DON'T TAKE THE WRAP

To ease the strain on refuse collection in remote areas, try to buy products with as little wrapping material as possible and discard any unnecessary packaging before you leave home.

813 DON'T FEED THE ANIMALS

Never feed wildlife or local pets when you're away from home and don't leave out food when you're abroad as it could encourage pests. If you really want to feed animals, visit a sanctuary or ask local guides for advice.

814 PROTECT THE REEFS

When you visit a coral reef or other natural site, help keep it healthy by respecting all local guidelines, recommendations, regulations, and customs. Ask the local authority or your dive store what measures you can take to help protect the reef.

815 STAY IN AN ECO-LODGE

Why not get into the green spirit on your vacation by staying in one of the many eco-lodges dotted around the globe. These are purpose-built to blend in with the environment and use as little external resources as possible.

816 DODGE ENDANGERED

Many tourist spots have local markets that can be fun to browse, but beware of animal products unless you can be sure they are not sourced from endangered species, particularly in the case of jewelry and carved products. If in doubt, don't buy.

817 UNDER FIRE

To prevent forest fires, don't light a match, cigarette, or other fire hazard in the wild. Once they start they're often impossible to contain, and can cause lasting damage to animal and plant life. Likewise, don't start open fires.

818 PEDAL POWER

Instead of driving on your next vacation, consider making it a bicycling trip. It will allow you to experience the countryside first hand, get you fit in the process, and of course minimize the effect of your break on the environment!

819 ADOPT AN ANIMAL

If you travel abroad and visit an animal sanctuary for wildlife like orangutans or elephants, think about adopting one of these animals. Your money could help that animal stay in the nature reserve and contribute toward saving others.

820 USE YOUR HOTEL

Your hotel or tour operator will have the contact details of local wildlife officers, so if you witness any suspicious wildlife activity, or see an animal that has been hurt, be sure to report it to them.

821 BE ALERT

If you witness any worrying incidents concerning animals while you are on vacation and can't report it to the local authorities, direct them to the "Travelers' Alert" online campaign of the Born Free Foundation, a worldwide charity aimed at stamping out animal cruelty and neglect (see www.bornfree.org).

822 GO LOCAL

On your next vacation, support the local economy by choosing a locally owned guest house or hotel rather than a multinational hotel chain. If you go for self-catering, buy food and drink in local stores rather than supermarket chains.

823 KNOW YOUR DESTINATION

To be sure you won't damage habitats when you travel, check your destination with organizations such as Conservation International (CI), dedicated to minimizing tourism effects on the environment, or the International Ecotourism Society (TIES), who promote responsible travel to natural areas.

824 TURN OFF YOUR AIR-CON

Don't forget to turn off the air conditioning in your hotel or guest house room when you aren't inside. Air conditioning is energy intensive, and what's the point of cooling a room you're not in?

825 BE A RESPONSIBLE TOURIST

If you're going to an endangered habitat area, choose a reputable tour operator like WWF. Then you can rest assured that they will be sensitive to protecting natural resources and wildlife and promote conservation.

826 EAT WITH CARE

Sampling local delicacies is an enjoyable part of many vacations, but make sure you're not contributing to the poaching or killing of protected wildlife species when you order wildmeat or bushmeat.

827 CHOOSE A GUIDE

Your experience will be far more authentic if you use licensed local guides, agents, and operators for your excursions and activities and not an international operator. It's also a great way to contribute to the local economy.

828 READ UP

If you're thinking about traveling to the Asia Pacific region, check out the International Ecotourism Society's (TIES) newsletter, which will point you in the direction of the greenest places.

829 KEEP THE LIGHTS LOW

Turn off the light when you leave your hotel room. Hotels are a hotbed of electrical activity so every little helps. Make a note to check that it's off before you close the door.

830 PAY TRAVEL A VISIT

VISIT (the Voluntary Initiative for Sustainability in Ecotourism) is a network of eco-labeling programs that has certified tour operators in many Western European countries. By choosing an operator who is part of VISIT, you'll be taking a step toward greener travel. See also National Geographic's Green Guide (www.thegreenguide.org) for more information.

831 ACTIVIST ACTION

Greenpeace is one of the world's best-known environmental activity groups and has organizations in most countries. You can donate money to help the natural world, but it's more fun to actually join them for activities and fundraising events.

832 LOOK BEFORE YOU BOOK

Before you book your hotel, get in contact and check what attempts the hotel makes to save energy. If you can, choose one with energy-saving devices such as timers or sensors on light switches—this means that lights wouldn't have to be left on all night in public areas.

833 TAKE AN ECO-BREAK

Think about what ecotourism means. Before you book your vacation, assess the impact you will have on the environment and how you can offset this damage by helping the local area to protect habitats and species.

834 JOIN THE ALLIANCE

The Rainforest Alliance has built partnerships with tour operators in 25 western hemisphere countries to set up a sustainable tourism network offering advice on safe tourism. Visit their website for details.

835 BRING IT HOME

Many remote areas where people go for vacation don't have the sort of recycling programs you may be used to at home. If possible, bring back home anything that can be recycled.

836 DON'T DROP LITTER

It is difficult and expensive to collect litter from remote areas like ski slopes and coastal areas, so avoid leaving garbage: you will help keep the area clean and attractive for others and help preserve natural habitats.

transportation & travel

837 WALK YOURSELF TO AN OLD AGE

Every mile you walk is estimated to add 20 minutes to your life. Walking is also the greenest transportation method, as every single journey in your car, taxi, bus, or train contributes to air pollution.

838 CONDITIONING RINSE

If your car has an air conditioner, make sure its coolant is recycled whenever you have it serviced. Ask your mechanic, or take it to a recycling program yourself.

839 GET ON THE BUS

One busload of people is worth 40 cars, so every time you step onto a full bus, that's minus 40 cars on the road and a staggering 9 tons of air pollution saved per year.

840 CHOOSE THE CHOO-CHOO

Trains are an environmentally friendlier way to travel than planes or cars, so choose them when you can for your vacations. Some trains allow you to take cars on board, or hire a car at your destination rather than driving the whole way.

841 SHARE THE DRIVE

Instead of having a car for your own use, join a car-sharing program locally or in your city, where you can book car time for a monthly fee. This reduces cars on the road and makes sure they are used efficiently.

842 LOVE TO LOBBY

Don't sit at home complaining about the state of trains and subways—take a positive step by lobbying local government to improve bus and bike lanes to encourage people to leave cars at home.

843 DON'T FLOOR IT

Your car functions most efficiently and is guzzling less gas when you go gently on the accelerator pedal. Pull away slowly for best fuel results. Driving more sensibly makes more sense for the environment as well.

844 DRIVE 2X2

Don't drive a four-wheel drive unless you really have to. Not only are they heavier than other cars, they also require more energy because the engine is driving four wheels. If you need one, at least go for one with both a two- and four-wheel drive option.

845 SMALL IS BEAUTIFUL

Don't go for a big car if you don't really need one. Buy the smallest, most energy-efficient car you can make do with to help reduce fuel costs and emissions.

846 HOORAY FOR HYBRIDS!

If you're thinking about replacing your car, lose the gas-guzzler and invest in a hybrid version. It uses a minimum amount of fuel, relying on a non-polluting fuel cell to provide some of the power electrically.

847 COAST TO COAST

Your car uses least fuel when the engine is ticking over and you're not using the accelerator or other pedals. Keep this in mind and coast up to red lights over a larger distance and drive more slowly rather than stopping and starting.

848 BETTER BIODIESEL

Look for vehicles and other machines that run on biodiesel, a naturally produced alternative to diesel fuel made from oils and greases. It does not harm the environment during use or manufacture.

849 IDLING AWAY

Turn off the engine when you stop your car in traffic—at slow traffic lights or roadworks. Leaving the engine to idle wastes gas and contributes to air pollution.

850 KEEP IT AERODYNAMIC

Don't drive with unnecessary accessories like roof racks or bars on top of your car, as these make the car less aerodynamic, meaning you will use more gas for the same journey.

851 DON'T PIMP YOUR RIDE

Even if you like the effect it has on passers-by, don't add flags or hanging toys to the outside of your car. Also remove logos and hood icons that stick up from the surface because they could reduce efficiency.

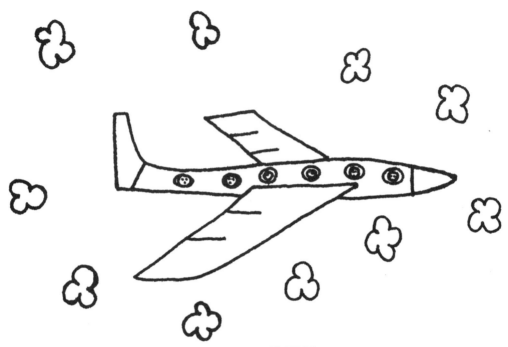

852 OFFSET YOUR EMISSIONS

Carbon offsetting is a way to neutralize the carbon emissions you emit when you drive or fly. You subscribe to an offsetting organization and donate money every time you travel—these funds then go toward planting trees and installing solar panels and wind turbines.

853 STAY AT HOME

Instead of heading off on a business trip every time you need to speak to overseas colleagues, help reduce greenhouse gas emissions by teleconferencing instead of flying. With modern technology such as video linking, it's almost like being in the same room.

854 CHECK YOUR OIL

Get your car oil checked regularly to prevent oil run-off due to leaky pipes or fittings in your engine. Car oil can damage the environment and wildlife if it leaks into drains, streams, and rivers.

855 WASH AND GO

Wash your car on the lawn. The soil underneath acts as a natural filter for the run-off, which can help fertilize your lawn. If you don't have a lawn, use a carwash. This prevents detergents, oil, and grease being washed into the storm drains and ending up in lakes, harbors, and beaches.

856 GO SMOOTH

Buy a more aerodynamic car to save fuel. Boxy cars that are high off the ground and square in shape are less aerodynamic than smooth, rounder silhouettes.

857 DON'T TIRE YOURSELF OUT

Buy high-quality or long-life tires instead of cheap versions that will wear out quickly. The high-quality versions actually cost less per mile traveled, and reduce the problem of disposing of worn out tires.

858 GET GREAT SERVICE

Service your car regularly to make sure your engine is running at its optimal level. This ensures the fuel you buy is being used as efficiently as possible, minimizing environmental effects.

859 PUMP IT UP

Check your tire pressure regularly to optimize performance and reduce your fuel emissions. Driving a car with incorrect air pressure in the tires can make it 10% less fuel efficient. Adjust the pressure according to the type of driving you're doing—loaded cars and fast highway driving require higher tire pressures.

baby care

860 BREAST IS BEST

If you have a young baby, the most environmentally friendly way to feed him or her is to breastfeed because it's energetically sound and doesn't require any external processes. There's no heating or sterilizing, and it's always available when needed!

861 FEED BABY ORGANICALLY

Choose organic baby food. Despite the baby food industry being carefully monitored, toxins from non-organic foods would be more difficult for babies' tiny systems to cope with, potentially causing more damage.

862 HOME AND AWAY

Some people find washable diapers a daunting prospect. Try working them into your life gently by using them only when you are at home, and using disposables when you're out or traveling—every little helps.

863 SOAKED TO THE SKIN

Instead of using chemical disinfectant or bleach on diapers, pre-soak in 3 tablespoons of baking soda dissolved in warm water in a sink or basin, or in the washing machine, for whiter-than-white results.

864 GREEN BABY

When you've finished with your baby food jars, don't throw them away. Instead, use them to freeze your own home-cooked foods so you can transport your baby's meals around easily. They can be washed and reused many times.

865 BE ALL RUBBERY

If you're worried about your baby or child wetting the bed at night, don't put plastic underneath them as it's bad for the environment and molecules may leach into the air. The healthier alternative is rubber.

866 GET A COLD CURE

For changing mats, choose latex that has been created using the cold cure technique. Latex is a natural product and entirely biodegradable.

867 HANDWASH HEROES

It has been estimated that 4% of domestic waste consists of used disposable diapers. One of the best choices you can make to reduce landfill and help the environment is to use washable diapers instead.

868 A HOME DELIVERY

If you aren't keen to spend your life by the washing machine but want to use washable diapers, consider joining a local diaper-washing service. They will take away the diapers once a week and return them to you clean and dry.

869 BIO BOTTOMS

If you want to use disposable diapers, go for a biodegradable version instead of the chemical-filled modern versions. Those made from wood pulp degrade more easily.

870 CHOOSE COTTON BOTTOMS

Instead of buying throw-away wipes when you change your baby, use organic cotton wool and warm water. They do just as good a job and are totally biodegradable.

871 SHUN THE SACKS

If you must use disposable diapers at least dispose of them without plastic sacks, which add yet more plastic to landfill sites. Never store diaper waste in bedrooms—be sure to discard every day.

872 BE HAPPY

If you're buying diaper disposal bags, make sure you buy biodegradable versions made from recycled materials. These won't stick around in landfill for hundreds of years like other plastic products.

873 WIPE AWAY WASTE

If you want to use baby wipes but are worried about waste, make your own wipes. Use cotton squares dipped in water mixed with vinegar, aloe vera, and a few drops of lavender or tea tree oil.

874 SOOTHE BABY'S SKIN NATURALLY

Petroleum-based baby oils and creams are harsh to manufacture and can block the skin's natural ability to breathe. Use natural oils like almond and olive oil instead.

875 DON'T DEGRADE YOURSELF

If you're choosing biodegradable diapers, think about disposing of them properly. High levels of methane and other gases in landfill sites slow down decomposition, so the best thing to do with biodegradable diapers is find somewhere to compost them.

876 GO MONOCHROME

Chrome, often used in the process of tanning leather, can be toxic to babies. Protect your baby as well as the environment from potential hazards by choosing chrome-free leather for baby shoes.

877 NO KIDDING AROUND WITH PLASTIC

Instead of feeding your children from plastic bowls, buy stainless steel versions. They'll last forever—and you can even use them for cat food when the kids have grown up!

878 DON'T BE BABY BLUE

Keep your baby or child's room free of electronic equipment to reduce electromagnetic radiation and static build-up, and make sure it is well ventilated to boost night-time health.

879 DRESS THE PART

Why not get other parents involved in a share group for clothing. This is especially useful if you all have children of various ages, as they will need different types of clothing at different times.

880 RECHARGE YOUR BATTERIES

Children's and babies' toys are heavy on batteries, particularly more modern toys with a variety of sounds and lights. Consider solar battery rechargers to boost the energy levels in your batteries without using too much electricity.

881 SHARE A TOY

Instead of buying large amounts of plastic toys, join a local toy share program where you can swap toys with other parents once a month. Your children won't get bored with the toys, but at the same time you're cutting down on wastage.

882 DON'T DRIVE BABY

Instead of sticking the baby in the car to get him or her to go to sleep, walk the little one around in a baby carrier or baby carriage instead to save air pollution from exhaust emissions.

883 WATER BABE

Soap can be harsh on a baby's soft skin. Use water alone to clean baby, unless the skin is really dirty or covered in cream or sunscreen. This way you'll reduce the amount of chemical-containing water that is flushed down into water systems.

kids & school

884 GIVE YOUR KIDS A HELPING HAND

If you're saving for your children's future by way of a government or private savings plan, make sure you start them off the right way by choosing an ethical policy or investing in companies that deliberately promote being green.

885 RUN A CAMPAIGN

Encourage your children's school to run an anti-litter awareness campaign by pointing out how damaging litter can be to local wildlife. Combine it with a litter-pick to clear up local parks or along highways.

886 GET ARTY

Encourage your children's school to recycle paper they use in the art room. For every ton of paper we reuse, 17 trees are spared.

887 JOIN A CLUB

Encourage your children to join an environmental club or local wildlife trust where they can learn about environmental hazards and how to protect and support wildlife. It's an excellent idea to have them participate in clean-up days.

888 GO NONTOXIC

Request a nontoxic environment in your child's school. Cleaning products, lawncare, teaching supplies and paint can all be switched for more environmentally friendly versions.

889 ASK FOR RECYCLING

Make a point of asking your school to recycle—not only food packaging and stationery supplies, but also other items such as unwanted shoes and clothes.

890 SHARE A SCHOOL RUN

If you have to drive your children to school, share the drive with another neighborhood family to save gas. You may decide to drive every other week or a set number of days per week.

891 THROW THE LICE

Headlice are becoming resistant to chemical shampoos designed to kill them. In addition, if you use them you're flushing insecticides down your drain. Make a conditioning rinse with your usual conditioner, vinegar, and tea tree oil, then comb through thoroughly once a week until the lice are gone.

892 MAKE IT A GAME

Help your children turn recycling into a game by letting them help you sort out the piles of items and take them to the recycling depot. Children love putting bottles into bottle banks and flattening cardboard, and it teaches them that recycling is a way of life.

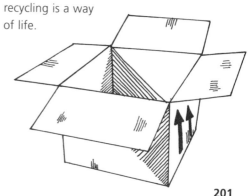

893 THINK OF THE CONSEQUENCES

Help your children understand the concept of waste minimization by measuring or weighing your family garbage at the end of the week before you sort it into recycling or disposal. Then show them how much landfill space you've saved by recycling.

894 DON'T LEAVE IT RUNNING

When you're collecting the children from school, don't leave your car engine running while you're waiting for them outside the school gates. Running engines emit greenhouse gases as well as elevate ground-level pollution. Switching off the car will save on your gas bill, too.

895 IN THE BAG

Instead of sending your children to school with individually wrapped snacks like potato chips or raisins every day, buy a large bag at the beginning of the week and add small portions to their lunchbox so you don't give them too much. You can also reuse small potato chip bags if you wash them out after use.

896 DON'T BE A LITTER BUG

If you send your children to school with food in packaging, give them bonus points for bringing it home. You will prevent littering on the playground, and you can recycle it at home.

897 LIMIT TV TIME

Limit the time your children are allowed to watch TV and play games, so electricity isn't wasted. Encourage them to spend more time doing outdoor activities and enjoying nature.

898 GET INTO BOXING

Instead of wrapping sandwiches in disposable plastic wrap, foil, or ziploc bags, invest in a metal sandwich box that you can reuse day after day to cut down on the waste you produce.

899 GROW THEIR OWN

Give your kids the chance to have their own patch in the garden. They can learn how to grow vegetables, or simply plant flowers to attract insects, worms, and other wildlife.

900 AHEAD OF THE GAME

Don't buy new computer games for your kids. Instead, borrow them from a library or rental store. This will reduce the amount of waste you produce and reduce your plastic quota, since most come in plastic cases. Find out about game-share programs running locally and online.

901 RENT A FILM

Instead of buying DVDs of your family's favorite films, rent them from a DVD rental store, website, or your local library. Even better, watch films on pay-per-view to cut out waste altogether.

902 USE WHAT YOU'VE GOT

Before rushing to the store to stock up on school supplies after summer is over, take a look at what you have left from the previous school year. Don't double up on anything.

903 WATER IT DOWN

Encourage your kids to drink water from a faucet or filter jug rather than highly packaged carbonated drinks or juice packs. If they do drink from plastic, make sure they know to recycle it or bring it home rather than throwing it away.

904 PROJECT THE FOREST

Why not start a rainforest project at school—raising money for your children's class in order to save an acre of rainforest is an exciting project that could involve them in green issues from a young age.

pets

905 ORGANIC NOURISHMENT

Choose pet food for your animals containing as much organic or fresh produce as possible, rather than multiprocessed alternatives that often contain little or no natural products. There is a good range of organic pet food, doggie biscuits, treats, and even homeopathic remedies available from natural pet stores.

906 PACK IT UP

Pet food packaging is often very wasteful, so choose products with as little packaging as possible and look for those packaged in cardboard or other recyclable materials rather than plastic. Choose as large packs as you can as they are more economical and use less packaging.

907 DON'T BE A LITTER BUG

Don't buy scented cat litter, which contains chemicals designed to be absorbed into the air. Buy unscented versions and look out for those made from recycled paper, cardboard, or whole-kernel corn.

908 GIVE THE DOG A BOWL

Don't let your cat or dog eat and drink from a plastic bowl, but choose a ceramic or stainless steel bowl instead. These are much less damaging to the environment in their manufacture and will last a lot longer, too.

909 DON'T PET SMUGGLERS

Rare or exotic pets, such as reptiles, birds, and snakes, are often smuggled or stolen from their natural habitat. If you buy one, make sure it's from a reputable pet store that can provide paperwork to prove that the animal was legally acquired. Before you buy, learn as much as you can about their natural habitat and endeavor to imitate it in the home you provide. Ensure you have ready access to adequate foodstuffs and specialist supplies that the pet requires.

910 SCOOP THE POOP

If you're being a good citizen by cleaning up after your dog on walks, choose recycled bags instead of plastic ones that don't biodegrade. If you can't find biodegradable doggie walk bags, use diaper disposal bags—they're the right size.

911 FISH CAREFULLY

Buy marine aquarium fish only if you know they have been collected in an ecologically sound manner. In some areas, marine fish harvested for the pet trade are stunned with sodium cyanide, which poisons reefs.

912 BETWEEN A ROCK AND A HARD PLACE

Don't start a "live rock" aquarium. Although living rock is still harvested legally in some places, its collection is devastating to the habitat of reef organisms, causing widespread loss of life.

913 RING YOUR CAT'S BELL

Make sure your cat wears a bell on its collar—the noise will warns birds to fly off, but mice and small rabbits might not get away so easily, so the cat can still be effective at getting rid of rodents.

914 COMB AWAY FLEAS

Don't sprinkle pesticide onto your pet's fur or use a flea collar. Instead, bathe it regularly using tea tree oil, then comb out any pests.

915 KEEP A KITTY

Keep your cat indoors overnight. Roaming house cats do tremendous damage to birds and other wildlife such as field mice, frogs, squirrels, and lizards and they can cover long distances in one night, so keeping them in is the best option.

leisure

916 DON'T PICNIC ON PLASTIC

Don't take plastic utensils on picnics. Instead, use old mugs and plates from your own home or buy a set from a charity shop or garage sale. Metal cutlery can be wrapped in a dish towel to stop it clunking around.

917 BE RESPONSIBLE

When fishing, make an effort not to disturb small animals. Remember not to use lead weights for angling as lead is a toxic metal. Make sure you discard hooks and nets responsibly or take them home with you as they are a potential threat to wildlife.

918 WAX YOUR CUPS

If you have to use disposable cups, opt for waxed paper, which can be recycled and is biodegradable, instead of polystyrene or plastic.

919 REUSE PLASTICS

If you have to use plastic cups, plates, or cutlery on picnics, don't throw them away. They can be used several times and even if you don't want to reuse them, you can donate them to charities who will.

920 THE DIRTY WORK

When you rent glasses for your next party, try to find a hire company that takes them back dirty and washes them. They will probably be washing in bulk so it will be more energy efficient than you doing it.

921 DOWNLOAD TRACKS

Instead of buying music CDs, download your music onto an MP3 player. Not only will you save on CD wastage, but you will also be able to take your whole music collection with you wherever you go. An MP3 player makes an ideal sound system for entertaining and discos.

recycling

922 RECYCLE FOR WILDLIFE

By recycling, you're helping to slow down the rate at which wild places are cut down, burned, and mined. The result is more habitat and food for wildlife and endangered species.

923 GET A COLLECTION

If you live in an area where recycling is not picked up and you're reluctant to make frequent trips to the bottle bank or recycling center yourself, find out if there's a local recycling program you can join. They may be able to collect all your recycling once a week.

924 LOOK FOR THE ARROWS

Choose recycled when it comes to fruit and vegetable packaging. Many supermarkets are catching on now—they're starting to realize that the consumer wishes to reduce their stacks of garbage, and are offering recycled and recyclable packaging. Look for the universally recognized recycle symbol.

925 STACK THEM HIGH

To encourage you to recycle at home, invest in stackable recycling receptacles. This will make it easier for you to separate your waste, without taking up too much space while you're collecting it.

926 GET BEHIND GLASS

Don't throw away glass jars—use them to store food in your home and to keep things airtight. Recycle both the glass jars and the metal lids when you can no longer use them.

927 RECYCLE THE PAPER

If you have to use paper towels, make sure you buy recycled and unbleached. Its manufacture does not pollute the environment as much.

928 IN THE CAN

Always recycle food and drink cans. Recycling aluminum requires only 5% of the energy it takes to process the original from the earth's crust. One-third of aluminum is currently reused, but it should be more.

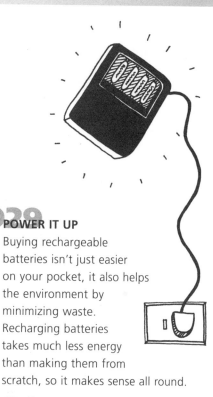

929 POWER IT UP

Buying rechargeable batteries isn't just easier on your pocket, it also helps the environment by minimizing waste. Recharging batteries takes much less energy than making them from scratch, so it makes sense all round.

930 DON'T DISPOSE

Whenever you can, swap your throw-away, disposable items for reusable versions. You won't have to pay out over and over again plus you'll avoid contributing to landfill.

931 BE A PAPER DOLL

Always recycle paper. Each time paper is recycled, the individual cellulose fibers become shorter. On average, a fiber can be recycled seven times before it is too short to combine with other fibers.

932 REMEMBER THE RECEIPTS

Don't forget that receipts can be recycled, too. It's easy to forget that receipts are paper and they can add up to quite a volume over time. If you're worried about divulging personal financial information, shred them first.

933 BOARD IT UP

A lot of food packaging is made of cardboard, so collect it at home and visit the recycling center regularly. Wax-coated cardboard milk or juice cartons, however, may need to be discarded with your regular trash. Check with your local township.

934 OIL YOUR RECYCLING

Make sure you recycle your motor oil rather than disposing of it. Oil can do serious damage to wildlife. Find a local recycling program or a garage that does it in bulk.

935 BAG THE BAGS

Plastic bags start as petrochemicals, which are transformed into polymers and are, in turn, heated, shaped, cooled, flattened, sealed, punched, and printed on, all of which require energy. But still only 0.6% of plastic bags are recycled, with the USA alone throwing away 100 billion bags a year. Make a difference by recycling.

936 RECYCLE APPLIANCES

If you're not selling them on, make sure you recycle your household appliances rather than throwing them away. Second-hand shops will often take them for parts, or ask your local government offices for advice on recycling programs. Big items are difficult and costly to dispose of and recycling centers will take them off your hands for free.

937 BAG A LIFE DEAL

Instead of throw-away plastic bags, think "reusable" when it comes to supermarket shopping. Many supermarkets now have "bag for life" programs or, even better, take your own.

938 GET SOME BOTTLE

It's really important to recycle your plastic bottles. They can be used to make other plastics, as well as a range of other materials including insulating fabrics and clothing.

939 CAN THE CAN

Recycling aluminum cans is a closed-loop system. Every can is infinitely recyclable and recyclers paid nearly $1 billion a year for aluminum beverage cans. The energy saved by recycling just one can is enough to run a TV set for three hours! If you have to use them, be sure to recycle.

940 GLASSY EYED

Glass is excellent for recycling because there are many different grades to work through before it reaches the point where it can no longer be recycled. Make sure you separate different colored glass and don't include metal bottle tops or corks that can contaminate the process.

941 CAN THE RUBBISH

Because metal doesn't break down easily and can be used to make a wide range of different items, metal food and drink cans are great for recycling.

942 GO GLOBAL

The Freecycle Network is a relatively new nonprofit online community with about two million members around the world. Their slogan, "Think globally, recycle locally," sums up their purpose. Members use the site to recycle perfectly good items that would otherwise be thrown away, working on the proviso that one man's trash is another man's treasure. Check it out online (www.freecycle.org). It is open to any individual who would like to participate.

943 REPAIR DON'T REPLACE

If your old washing machine or dryer isn't working, see if you can get it repaired rather than throwing it away and buying a new one. Most parts are easy to replace.

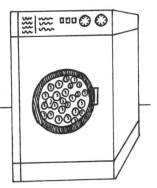

water

944 PLUMB THE LINE

Incorrect plumbing in the home could mean that wastewater from dishwashers, washing machines, sinks, showers, and even toilets is flushed directly into your local river. Misconnected pipes are a common cause of pollution to rivers and streams, especially in urban areas. Make sure your external drainage pipes are not misconnected.

945 LITTER AWAY

Keep litter, pet waste, and leaves out of street gutters and storm sewers that drain into natural water habitats. Pet waste contain bacteria and viruses that can threaten fish, wildlife, and human health.

946 SAVE OUR SEAS

You might think oceans are not affected by water use in your home, but think again. The ocean is, in fact, one of the hardest-hit habitats because wastewater and run-off eventually find their way back there, causing pollution. So saving water saves the seas.

947 DON'T SOIL YOUR SEWERS

Cover piles of sand, soil, or mulch in your garden to stop them washing into the sewer when it rains. These substances can block drains, leading to water wastage when water diverts to other routes.

948 GET GROUPING

When you're planning your garden and trying do decide what to plant where, group plants with similar water needs together. Some plants might need water every night in the summer, but others can go without watering for a week or two. Grouping them this way means you won't be wasting water on plants that don't need it.

949 DRAIN IT AWAY

Keep storm sewers clean—they drain off to watersheds, canals, beaches, and rivers so blockages, pollutants, or litter in them will eventually find their way into natural habitats, causing problems for plant and animal life. Storm water that flows into drains is not treated and filtered for pollutants, and it can get into the drinking water supply, too.

950 CARWASH CURE

Don't waste water washing your car. Wait until it rains, let nature do it for you and simply wipe with a chamois afterward to clear up smears and water marks.

951 SAVE SOME WATER

Millions of gallons of water are wasted every year because of leaks—not only in the home but also by water companies. Lobby your water company to make sure they're running proper maintenance checks on their equipment.

952 PULL THE TRIGGER

Use a trigger nozzle on your hosepipe when you use it to water your garden. Targeting water only where it's needed ensures you don't waste any where it's not absolutely necessary.

953 FEED THE METER

Installing a water meter in your home is a great step forward. Once you start measuring your water usage, you'll become more aware of waste and it will force you to think of ways to save water.

954 GET A BALANCE

Save water by getting the water balance of your swimming pool right. You won't have to keep adding water and you'll save money on chemicals as well.

955 COVER UP

Use a swimming pool cover to reduce evaporation and therefore water loss. This can save more than half the water in your pool over a year.

956 THROW IT AWAY

Use your wastebasket for miscellaneous bathroom wastes instead of flushing them down the toilet.

957 TURN IT OFF

Don't leave the faucet running while brushing your teeth or shaving. Get into the habit of turning it off unless you're actually using it.

958 FIX THE DRIP

Do a water inventory in your house and fix any leaking faucets—over time even a small drip can add up to a lot of waste.

wildlife

959 GIVE BACK A DAY

Nature reserves need to be managed by humans to stay in the best condition. Volunteer for a day's work at your local reserve. Often, this can be done through local organizations and even one day of your time can make a huge difference to accomplishing something for local plant and animal welfare.

960 DOWN ON THE FARM

Many farmers would like to help habitats develop but are under too much financial pressure. Lobby your state government for measures, such as grants and one-off incentives, to encourage farmers to save natural habitats.

961 FOXGLOVE FUN

Bees like white, blue, and yellow flowering plants with deep flowers and lots of nectar. Foxgloves and hollyhocks are great bee favorites, so try and plant some in your garden. Encouraging natural habitats helps support the ecosytem.

962 SAY NO TO GM

It's still not quite clear what effect GM crops have on wildlife, but the expert consensus seems to be that genetic modification can adversely affect biodiversity and can damage the delicate balance of ecosystems.

963 HAVE A RIVER DAY

Volunteer to spend a day with your local wildlife rangers helping replant river banks with native plants. These areas are under threat because of pollution but they support hundreds of species, so you'll be giving wildlife a helping hand.

964 PLANT A WILDLIFE GARDEN

Encourage your local school to develop a wildlife garden that will attract wild insects and birds. Once it is established, it will give children an excellent opportunity to study wildlife behavior.

965 BOLT UP A BEE BOLTHOLE

Drill holes in a block of untreated wood and hang it under the eaves of your house or garden shed to provide a bee shelter where solitary bees can rest and make their home. Make sure it's protected from wind, sun, and rain.

966 BUTTERFLY BUSH

Adult butterflies need plants like buddleia in the garden to provide nectar. What many people don't know is that they also need water, so attract them to your garden by filling a shallow dish, or a rock or tree hollow, with water.

967 BASK IN THE SUNLIGHT

Attract butterflies to your summer garden by adding a light-colored rock or garden sculpture. This provides a surface for basking in the early-morning sun. Make it a few feet high for protection against predators.

968 GIVE BIRDS A DRINK

In the summer months it can be hard for birds to find water to drink and wash in. As well as leaving them food, make sure you leave some water as well.

969 BOX YOUR BATS

If you have space in your backyard, help the local wildlife by putting up a bat box. Bats are natural predators of night-flying insects like moths and flies, and will help keep your patio, porch, or deck insect-free on summer evenings.

970 KEEP UP THE CORRIDORS

Wildlife in built-up areas need corridors of habitat to get from one green space to another. Protest against building on these spaces and preserve greenery in your area.

971 DON'T FLY THE NEST

Leave bird nests alone—birds are highly sensitive to smells and if they can scent a stranger's aroma on or near their nest, they're likely to abandon it and might not re-breed.

972 HOME MOVIE

To really make the most of wildlife in your garden, invest in a bird box with a pinhole camera inside. They transmit images to your own TV set so the whole family can watch them day and night and see the chicks grow up.

973 BOX UP A BIRD HOME

Why not add a few nestboxes to your garden to provide a nesting site and shelter for birds. Choose a tree or a high wall, but avoid sunny spots or anywhere accessible to cats or foxes. Be patient—it may take a season before the nestbox is settled and the birds make it their home.

974 LEAVE IT TO THE EXPERTS

Do not attempt to raise or keep wild animals yourself. Not only is it illegal, but wild creatures do not make good pets—captivity poses a constant stress, stopping them from developing normally. They are usually unable to be returned to the wild. Contact a wildlife organization for advice.

975 DON'T TOUCH

As a general rule, leave infant wildlife alone. A parent may be nearby or will return soon but may not do so if you have interfered with their young. The only exception is baby birds that have fallen from the nest, in which case you can gently return them using a towel or cloth.

976 CAP YOUR FLUES

Place caps over all chimneys and vents on your roof to prevent birds, ducks, and mammals like squirrels and raccoons from taking up residence and becoming a nuisance or getting trapped.

977 CHOOSE LIFE

Before you fell a tree in your garden, check carefully that no wildlife species are using it as a home or nesting in it, especially around springtime, when many birds are building nests and laying eggs.

978 DON'T MOW

Before mowing your lawn, walk through the area first to make sure no rabbits or ground-nesting birds are in harm's way. It only takes a couple of weeks for these babies to grow and leave the nest, so don't mow if you see them.

979 STAND YOUR GROUND

As long as your trees aren't diseased, consider leaving dead trees standing rather than cutting them down, as dead wood will provide a welcome home for many types of wildlife.

980 DRIVE CAREFULLY

Be alert when driving in rural areas or near wildlife refuges to avoid hitting or running over wild creatures. Animals do not recognize the danger from an oncoming vehicle so it's important you allow them time to move out of the way.

981 TEACH THEM WELL

Educating children to respect and care for all wild creatures and their habitats is important. They'll understand why nests, burrows, and other wildlife homes should never be destroyed, and that wild animals and birds should not be trapped or touched.

982 SEEING IS BELIEVING

Binoculars are a great choice for wildlife watchers who respect wild animals. They enable you to see close up what's happening without invading the animal's territory or scaring it away. Zoom lenses are also good for this. Make sure you do not make any loud noises, are wearing suitable clothing, and are respectful of the wildlife.

983 ADOPT SOME SPACE

If you haven't got room for a wildlife sanctuary in your own garden, why not adopt an area of local habitat nearby? Several conservation organizations have programs by which you can directly help protect an area of wild local habitat.

984 BE A RAINFOREST ANGEL

You can become a guardian of the Amazon by donating money to the World Wildlife Fund. It will go toward setting aside land in the Amazon for protection and towards teaching the local people how to watch over it. Visit the World Wildlife Fund website to find out about more ways you can help: www.wwf.org.

985 STEP IT UP

If you have areas of open water on your property, such as a pond or water feature, make sure you have steps or a structure that is easy to climb up. Many different wild animals die each year after getting stuck in ponds and artificial water features. Rocks are a great natural way to ensure they have a way out.

986 LEAVE THEM ALONE

Prevent your pet cats and dogs from attacking or playing with wildlife. Don't allow them to run without supervision and raise your cats as indoor pets. Many wild animals are injured each year by domestic dogs and cats.

987 RAISE A GLASS

To stop collisions, alert birds to large expanses of glass in your home, such as patio doors or picture windows, and cut down on reflection by hanging streamers, putting bird silhouettes on the glass surface, or allowing the glass to get a little dirty.

988 GIVE WILDLIFE A BREAK

One of the biggest problems for wildlife is habitat loss, so why not create a habitat in your own garden? Make a bird or butterfly sanctuary in your garden. Put up bird feeders for seed-eating birds like finches, jays, and sparrows. If you grow the right flowering plants you'll also provide nourishment for nectar-eating birds such as hummingbirds and orioles.

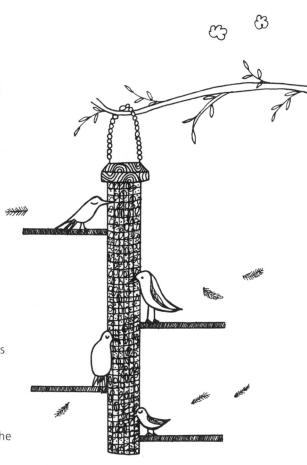

989 LEAVE FLOWERS TO GROW

PIcking flowers from the wild can lead to wildlife habitat denigration as they often don't grow back. Try to enjoy them where they grow.

990 DON'T DROP THE BAG

Potato chip and snack bags are a potential suffocation hazard to wild mammals. They lick the bags to get the high levels of salt, but when the bags get stuck on their noses they can't breathe.

991 DON'T BE FISHY

Do not leave fishing line or fish hooks unattended or lying outside because it may be harmful to animals and plants. Similarly, try to retrieve any kite string left on the ground or entangled in trees.

992 DON'T OIL YOUR PANS

Never leave motor oil unattended and uncovered. Birds can easily fall into containers and, because the oil destroys their natural feather oils, few survive such an ordeal.

993 CLEAN UP WILD HABITATS

When you visit a beach, park, or camping area, clean up any litter, especially if it's been around food. The scent may fool animals into thinking that aluminum foil, plastic bags, and other food containers are food. When eaten, these may cause them serious harm.

994 CUT UP YOUR RINGS

Always cut up the plastic that holds your four-pack or six-pack of beer before you throw it away. The rings can cause severe damage to wild birds through strangulation and can also get caught on dolphins' noses, leading to suffocation.

995 KEEP YOUR DOG ON A LEASH

If you're walking your dog in an area that contains wildlife, keep it under control or on a leash. Dogs can disturb ground-nesting birds to the point of abandoning their nests. The same applies on beaches, where they can disturb seashore animals.

996 RUN A REPORT

If you come across an abandoned car, report it to the police immediately as it could be a potential hazard to wildlife, especially if it catches fire.

997 KEEP IT QUIET

Did you know noise travels farther at night because of the colder layer of air near the earth? Turn the volume down a notch to ensure you're not scaring wild animals at night.

998 MAKE SOME MONEY

Organize a sponsored event or sale at your school or club to raise money to help preserve wildlife habitats, either locally or across the globe, through a charitable organization.

999 SET THE FUR FLYING

Don't wear fur. Fur farms are intensively reared and trapping wild animals for fur is a definite no-no for conservation, as it has serious animal cruelty issues and can endanger species.

1000 GOING TO THE ZOO

Become a member of your local aquarium or zoo, but only if they have conservation programs and are helping wild animals or endangered habitats to survive. Your joining fee will contribute toward those programs.

1001 BE A LITTER PICKER

Pick up litter that could harm wildlife, and take special care with items that pose a tangling or suffocation risk like bits of string, rope, plastic wrap, or plastic bags.

INDEX

action pumps 10, 145
additives 166
adobe walls 33
aerosols 145, 146
air conditioning 29, 90, 188, 191
air fresheners 10, 12
air pollution 19, 41, 60, 105, 125, 180, 191
air travel 182, 183, 194
alarm clocks 73
aloe vera 171
aluminum 209
  foil 79, 81, 84
animal adoption 179
antibiotics 157, 161
ants 44
appliances 81, 87, 89, 210
arnica 172
aromatherapy 147

baby care 196–200
baby food 196, 197
bacteria 78
bamboo 36, 39, 60
band-aids 173
bandages 173
bath oils 143
bathrooms 60–70
  fans 68, 69
baths 61, 62, 63, 67, 212
bats 216
batteries 39, 209
  chargers 48
beauty matters 140–46
bedding 71, 72, 73
bedrooms 71–3
beds 72
bee shelters 215
bidets 66
binoculars 218
bird tables 99
birds 168, 215, 216, 217, 219
bleaches 9, 55
blenders 88
boilers 29, 50
borax 19

Born Free Foundation 187
bottles 41, 152, 211
brass 14
bread 166
breastfeeding 196
bricks, recycled 33
bulk buying 133
buses 191, 192
businesses 122–9
butterflies 216, 219

calculators 133
cameras 180
candles 39, 90
carbon footprint 43, 124, 129
cardboard 210
cards 178
carpets 14, 20, 30, 31, 39, 92, 130
cars 181, 191, 192–3, 195, 201, 202, 213
cats 219
CDs 130, 135, 207
ceiling fans 29, 126, 131
cell phones 127, 136
  chargers 40
cellophane 79
CFCs (chlorofluorocarbons) 82
charities 176, 184
chewing gum 15, 168
children and school 200–203
chimneys 22
chlorine 173
chocolate 163
chrome 14, 199
cigarette smoking 39, 40, 174
cleaning/maintenance contractors 122
clothing 56, 57, 58, 147–52, 199
cockroaches 44
coffee 162
commuting 122, 123, 125, 126
companies see businesses
composite materials 133
compost 64, 103, 105–7
computer disks 136
computer games 203

computer mice, infra-red 135
computers 125, 130–33, 135, 136, 139
conditioners 145
Conservation International (CI) 188
conservatories 32, 36
copper 14
coral 178, 182, 184, 186
cork 21, 27
correction tape/fluid 135
cosmetics 140, 141, 143
cotton 148, 172, 178
creosote 101
curtains 25, 30, 48, 68, 90
cutting boards 88
cycling 123, 124, 187, 192

daylight 34, 43, 130
deforestation 75, 100
degreasing, kitchen 10, 14
dental fillings 171
deodorants 145
Derris 119
desks 133, 134
detergents 9, 10, 53, 58, 69
diapers 196, 197, 198
diatomaceous earth 121
digging 103
digital photographs 139
dishcloths 8
dishwashers 56, 59, 212
disinfectants 9, 12, 175
dogs 219, 221
double glazing 36
drains/sewers 15, 213
drafts 25, 31, 34, 41, 62, 73, 90
drink see food and drink
drink cans 209, 211
dust covers 37
dusters 40
duvets 71, 72
DVDs 203
dyeing 56
dyes 145, 149, 150, 161

e-cloths 89
eco cleaners 66
eco houses 33
eco-burials 177
eco-lodges 186
ecotourism 190
eggs 158
electromagnetic equipment 40, 92
emails 132, 137, 139
empty calories 166
endangered species 186
energy, sustainable 48
energy audit 124
envelopes 127, 137, 138, 178
essential oils 143
ethical investments 176
ethical mortgages 176
exercise 168–70

fabric softeners 54
farmers' markets 152
faucets 48, 58, 67, 70, 78, 125, 155, 167, 168, 214
feeding bowls 199
fertilizers 108, 117, 155, 157
fiberglass 62
filing cabinets 134
filters 41
  coffee 127
fires 22–5
forest 186
fish 157, 160–61
fishing 206, 220
fixers, reusable 126
flame-retardant chemicals 74
flashlights 42
flat screens 132
fleas 47, 101
flies 44, 45, 46, 107
flooring
  green alternatives 37, 60, 90, 181
  linoleum 20
  natural fabrics 2
  reclaimed granite or slate 21
  stone 21

vinyl 20
  wood 10, 20, 21, 34
flues, capping 217
fluorine 173
flypaper 45
food and drink 152–68
food cans 209, 211
formaldehyde 76, 147
formica 76
Freecycle Network 212
freezers 81, 83, 84, 85
fresh air 169, 170
fresh food 152, 154, 156, 160
fruit 114, 153, 155, 156, 162, 167
fungicides 17, 19
fur 221
furniture 74–7
  garden 100, 101
futons 71

garbage bags 42, 43
garden seats 99
garden tools 115
gas cookers 84
gifts 178, 179, 180
glass 33, 164, 166, 173, 209,
  211, 219
glasses (drinking) 207
glasses (spectacles) 175
gloves 122
glues 134
glutaraldehyde disinfectants 175
GM (genetically modified)
  products 162, 215
gold 179
golf courses 168
granite 89
gray water 59, 95
green decisions 176–7
Greenpeace 190
grills 100
grow-bags 112

hair
  dyes 145
  washing 70, 142

hand-rub gels, alcohol-based
  175
hardwoods 21
hay/straw bales 33
hayboxes 87
headlice 201
health and hygiene 168–75
heating 22–36
  central 25–9
  electric 25
  fires 22–5
  insulation 30–31
  solar power 30, 32, 34–5
hedges 99
hemp 74, 148
herbal teas 161
herbicides 168
herbs 161, 163
home energy audit 50
home office 129–36
hosepipes 213
humidity 92, 131
hygiene see health and hygiene

incineration 128
insecticides 44, 46, 201
insulation 20, 29–31, 33, 36, 37,
  40, 50, 73, 84
International Ecotourism Society,
  The (TIES) 188, 189
iron scorches 16
iron-resistant fabrics 147
irrigation systems 108, 111

junk mail 37

kettles 83, 86
kitchen gadgets 88
kitchens 78–88
  implements 81

labels 180
lampshades 39, 90
latex 197
laundry detergent 52
lawns 94–7, 217

LCD displays 48
leather 147, 199
leisure 206–7
lettuce 163
light bulbs 9, 49, 90
lighting 43, 50, 69, 90, 93
  business 125, 126, 131
  hotels 189, 190
  outdoor lights 97
limestone 98
limewash 19
linseed oil 17, 101
lipstick 141
litter 190, 200, 202, 221
local food 152, 153, 154, 156
lubricants 20
lunch boxes 128

magazines 137, 181
magnetic washing ball
  54
mascaras 142
masks 18
mattresses 72
MDF (medium-density
  fiberboard) 76
meat 157, 161
medicines 173, 174
melamine 76
menstrual cup 171
mercury 43, 171
mice 47
microwave ovens 88–9,
  166
milk 161, 166
mineral deposits 67
moisturizers 144, 146
mops 78, 124
mosquitoes 47
mosses 103
moths 45, 46, 47
motor oil 220
moulis 88
mouse mats 135
mulch 108, 116
multitasking 48

natural resources 178
nematodes 118
newspapers 37, 127, 137, 139

organic box schemes 155
ovens 84–7
  microwave 88–9
ozone 130

packaging 10, 69, 114, 137,
  140, 153, 157, 162, 164, 165,
  166, 170, 175, 182, 186, 201,
  204, 210
parchment paper 79
paints 17, 19, 22, 60, 100, 130
pans 9, 79, 81, 86
paper 134, 137–9, 210
paper towels 209
patios 100
pencils 127
pens 135
perfumes 140, 142
pesticides 39, 44, 46, 116, 117,
  119, 120, 155, 161, 168, 205
pests 44–7, 107, 116–21, 186,
  205
pets 186, 204–5
pharmaceutical companies
  172, 173
phosphates 52
phosphonates 52
phthalates 140, 141
pillows 72
pipes
  copper 30, 34
  drainage 212
  lagging 39
plant containers 99, 112, 114
plants 12, 18, 92, 93, 101–4,
  108–115, 129, 144, 180, 184,
  213 and pests 116–21
plaster 33
plastic 78, 89, 164, 206
  bags 164, 181, 182, 210
  cups 127, 168, 207
plastic wrap 79, 166

INDEX

polishes 8, 13
ponds 98, 118, 218
potato chip bags 220
potatoes 113
pots and pans 79
printer cartridges 133
printers 130, 139
processed foods 167
PVC (polyvinyl chloride) 20, 21,
   133, 166, 174
pyrolysis 128

quilts, patchwork 151

radiation, electromagnetic 40, 48,
   129, 131, 132, 133, 199
radiators 25, 26, 28, 56
radios 186
rainforest 203
Rainforest Alliance 190
rainwater 95, 111
rats 47, 107
rayon 147
razors 146
recycled symbol 66
recycling 128, 133–9, 152, 178,
   190, 191, 200–203, 208–212
refrigerators 43, 80–85
reupholstery 75
reusable articles 39, 76, 173, 209
rocks 98, 218
rodent poison 46
roof insulation 50
rugs 92

sandwich boxes 202
sanitary napkins 170,
   171
schools 200–203
screening 97
seagulls 107
seasonal foods 152, 156
secondhand purchases 38
sewerage systems, reed-bed 33
shampoos 69, 145, 201

shoes 147, 168
shopping 178–82
showers 62, 64, 67, 68, 70
shrubs 99
silk 55, 149
silver cleaners 8, 14
silverfish 46
sinks 212
six-pack rings 221
skiing 184–5
skincare 143, 144
sleep 174
sleep function 132
smells, neutralizing 10, 12
soap 14, 52, 117, 121, 143,
   146, 178, 200
socks, boiling 55
sofas 74
soil 105, 108
solar cookers 87
solar power 30, 32, 34–5, 51
solvents 18, 22, 58, 127
spiders 46, 117
sponges 65
stainless steel 89
stains 12, 14, 15, 16, 53, 55
standby 133
stickers 134
suit covers 56
supersizes 164, 165
surfactants (APEs and LAS) 52
swimming pools 214

tabletops 76
talcum powder 175
tampons 170, 171
tea 161, 162
tea tree oil 171, 205
teak, recycled 21
teleconferencing 194
telecommuting 122
television 132, 139, 202, 211
tents 181
textile banks 152
thermostats 25, 26, 27, 28
tiki torches 98

tiles 67, 68, 76
timber, reclaimed 97
toilets 11, 64–5, 66, 126, 212
   brushes 66
   paper 67
toothbrushes 41, 66, 67
toothpaste 175
top ten little ways to save
   the planet 6–7
tourism 182–90
towels 62, 70, 184
toys 199
trains 192
transport and travel 191–5
trays, desk 134
treadmills 168
trees 102, 137, 180, 200, 217
tumble dryers 57, 212

utilities companies 50, 51

varnish substitute 17
vegetables 113, 115, 153,
   155, 162, 164, 167, 203
ventilation 41, 78, 130
vinyl 20, 166
VISIT (Voluntary Initiative
   for Sustainability in
   Ecotourism) 190
VOCs (volatile organic
   compounds) 36, 131

walking 123, 180, 191, 200
wall hangings 40
wallpapers 20, 40
walls, weatherproofed 50
washing and drying 52–9
washing machines 54, 56,
   59, 212
water 212–14
   drinking 167, 180, 203, 216
water features 98, 118, 218
water filters 41, 93
water meters 213
water pollution 33
watermarks 16

weeds 116
weevils 46, 47
wild flowers, picking 220
wildflower meadows 109
wildlife 184, 186, 187, 189,
   203, 206, 208, 214–21
wildlife gardens 215
wills 176
wind power 51
windbreaks 98
window-cleaning 10
wine 153, 163
wood 74, 100, 133, 178
   fires 22, 23, 24
   paneling 22, 60
   preservative 101
wood-burning stoves 22, 23,
   24, 29
wool 150
worktops 76
World Wildlife Fund (WWF)
   129, 179, 188, 218
wormeries 106
wounds 172

ACKNOWLEDGMENTS

Thank you to Kevin Hall and
Pauline Floyd for their support,
the Sussex Wildlife trust and
Magpie Recycling Scheme in
Brighton for advice and Lisa
Dyer of Carlton Books for always
having a smile on her face!
Without the opportunity to write
this book I'd still be throwing
away my foil, so I'm grateful for
the chance to change my ways
before it's too late.